"This is a *fun* book! With all the 'compost' in the diet book industry, the compost the Dynamic Gardening Way recommends is finally something you can really benefit from."

—C. Wayne Callaway, M.D.
Clinical associate professor of medicine
George Washington University
Author of *The Callaway Diet*

"Too often, we are caught up in the fads and quick-fix road to wellness. Jeff Restuccio has formulated a fascinating and sound program to achieve true fitness of body, mind and environment.

"I particularly like his no-nonsense approach to exercise. He incorporates functional flexibility and strength training, using easily constructed backyard structures and time-tested exercises that combine his love of the outdoors, the earth, and good old-fashioned physical exertion.

"Anyone embracing this vision and following this well-conceived program will lead a wholesome, vigorous and rewarding lifestyle."

—Charles C. Norelli, M.D.
Good Shepherd Hospital

"*Fitness the Dynamic Gardening Way* is not just another book about gardening or fitness "techniques." Instead, it offers a broad perspective that serves to remind us that growing food, physical exercise and care of the planet are, in actuality, one interconnected, human activity."

—Saki Santorelli, M.A.
Associate Director, Stress Reduction Clinic
University of Massachusetts Medical Center

"Jeff has come up with a plan which combines gardening techniques that *get* you fit, and the fitness techniques that produce the kind of high-quality, nutritious foods that will *keep* you fit. Now, that's *really* cross-training."

—Mike McGrath
Editor-in-Chief
Organic Gardening Magazine

"Dynamic Gardening is a wonderful and healthy way for people to take personal responsibility for what happens in their life."

—Susan Olson, Ph.D.
Clinical Psychologist

"Gardening *can* become a permanent lifestyle change for weight management."

—Hope Weisel, M.S., R.D.
St. Luke's Roosevelt Hospital Center
Weight Control Unit

"Everyone who gardens has experienced the personal healing and growth that comes with nurturing plants. This dynamic book will appeal to a broad spectrum of individuals and groups who wish to use gardening as a tool to improve their physical and psychological well-being—whether they be parents or teachers concerned with improving the health and self-esteem of children, older adults who seek enabling methods to reduce stress, increase physical exercise and sensory stimulation, or health and human service practitioners serving disabled and disadvantaged populations through horticultural therapy. The author's innovative health and wellness program is bound to inspire readers to 'stretch' themselves mentally and physically, in and out of the garden."

—Nancy C. Stevenson, HTR
President
American Horticultural Therapy Association

Why is *Fitness the Dynamic Gardening Way* unique?

It's the **first**:

❀ *fitness book* that introduces a specific health and wellness *lifestyle,* integrating exercise, sound nutrition, and stress relief.

❀ *exercise book* that includes stretching, aerobics and resistance training as a *side-benefit* of growing fresh fruits and vegetables.

❀ *diet book* that explains how to get fresher, less expensive, better-tasting, and more nutritious fruits and vegetables.

❀ *weight-loss program* which measures its success in seasons, years and decades.

❀ *fitness how-to book* that explains not only the "how to" but the "why."

❀ *self-help book* that uses gardening to build self-esteem, keep fit, assert "positive affirmations" and relieve stress.

❀ *environmental book* that helps *you* be healthier while helping the environment.

❀ *gardening book* that combines gardening, exercise, nutrition, and psychology into a recipe for lifelong health and wellness.

Fitness

the

Dynamic Gardening Way

A Health and Wellness Lifestyle

by Jeffrey P. Restuccio

Balance of Nature Publishing, Cordova, Tenn.

As with any physical activity, the danger of injury is always present with improper application. The author assumes no liability for injuries resulting from the use of this book. It should not be used as a substitute for the advice of a physician. Please consult with your physician before engaging in this or any other diet and exercise program.

Fitness the Dynamic Gardening Way
Balance of Nature Publishing

First Printing, April 1992
All Rights reserved.

For information, contact Balance of Nature Publishing, P. O. Box 637, Cordova TN 38018-0637

Copyright © 1992 by Jeffrey P. Restuccio

Publisher's Cataloging in Publication
(Prepared by Quality Books Inc.)

Restuccio, Jeffrey P.
Fitness the dynamic gardening way : a health and wellness lifestyle / by Jeffrey P. Restuccio.
p. cm.
1-880886-10-3
Includes bibliographic references and index.

1. Physical Fitness—Exercise. 2. Organic gardening—Health aspects—United States. 3. Horticulture. I. Title

SB453.5.R4 1992   635.0484
QBI91-1912

Library of Congress Catalog Card Number: 92-70027
$12.95 softcover
Printed in the United States of America

Table of Contents

1. A New Approach to Fitness   13

PART ONE: Current Diet and Exercise Programs
2. Why Diets Fail   23
3. Why Exercise Programs Fail   35

PART TWO: Lifestyle
4. Lifestyle Not Changed   39
5. The Dynamic Gardening Way   45

PART THREE: Exercise
6. The Exercise Program   55
7. Circuit Training   81
8. Analysis by Muscle Groups   105
9. Five-Year Exercise & Gardening Plan   113

PART FOUR: Sustainable Gardening
10. Sustainable and Intensive Gardening Techniques   121
11. Composting and Raised Bed Gardening   125
12. Integrated Pest Management and
    Sustainable Gardening   141
13. Plant Propagation   157
14. Seasons   167

PART FIVE: Sound Nutrition
15. Fresh Fruits and Vegetables   179
16. Proper Preparation   195

PART SIX: The Role of the Mind
17. Beyond Diet and Exercise   199
18 "Sounds Interesting, But . . . ."   205
19. Stress   215
20. Horticultural Therapy   219
21. Visualization   231
22. Gardening by Objectives   237

PART SEVEN: Children
23. Gardening with Children   247

PART EIGHT: Summary

24. A Day in the Garden   255

25. Summary   261

PART NINE: Appendix

A. Sources for Supplies   266

B. Selected Bibliography   273

C. Index   281

Preface

Fitness the Dynamic Gardening Way is the result of two-and-a-half years of research and interviews with dozens of the nation's leading exercise physiologists, weight-loss specialists, psychologists, nutritionists and horticultural therapists.

The Dynamic Gardening Way expands and integrates the exercise, nutritional and psychological benefits of gardening.

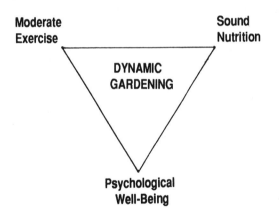

I suggest you first skim through this book noting the chapters that interest you. Don't get bogged down on any particular detail. Throughout this book I introduce hundreds of suggestions on how to integrate gardening into your current lifestyle. Many of the ideas I present will challenge long-standing notions of fitness. By the time you're finished, I feel you'll have an entirely new perspective on how gardening can help you live a healthier, happier life.

Acknowledgements

I thank the following for their contributions to this book:
Bruce Ames, Ph.D., Department of Biochemistry, University of California at Berkeley CA.

Jeffrey Blumberg, Ph.D., professor of nutrition and chief, Antioxidants Research Laboratory, Tufts University, Boston MA.

Darrin Brooks, certified athletic trainer and supervisor of sports medicine, Methodist Hospital, Memphis TN.

C. Wayne Callaway, M.D., assistant professor of medicine, George Washington University, Washington DC. Author of *The Callaway Diet*.

Harold Cardwell, HTR, Florida Division of Blind Services, Rehabilitation Center, Daytona FL.

Nancy Chambers, HTR, director, and Patrick Neal Williams, M.S., HTR., Enid A. Haupt Glass Garden, Howard A. Rusk Institute of Rehabilitation Medicine, N.Y.U. Medical Center.

Earl Copus, director, Melwood Horticultural Training Center, East Marlboro MD.

Gordon Cummings, second dan, martial arts instructor, Cordova TN.

Gilbert B. Forbes, M.D., University of Rochester Medical School, Rochester NY.

David Garner, Ph.D., professor, department of psychiatry, Michigan State University, East Lansing MI.

Philip Garry, Ph.D., University of New Mexico Medical School, Albuquerque NM.

Lloyd J. Kraft, National Men's Garden Clubs/Chairman, *Gardening From the Heart*.

Bibby Moore, HTR, coordinator of the horticultural therapy program at the North Carolina Botanical Garden and author of *Growing With Gardening*.

Charles Norelli, M.D., Good Shepherd Rehabilitation Hospital, Allentown, PA.

Susan Olson, Ph.D., clinical psychologist, Scottsdale, AZ, and author of *Keeping it Off*.

Paula Diane Relf, H.T.M., Ph.D., extension specialist, Department of Horticulture, Virginia Tech., Blacksburg VA.

Saki F. Santorelli, M.A., associate director, Stress Reduction and Relaxation Program, University of Massachusetts Medical Center, Worcester MA.

Susan Schiffman, Ph.D., Department of Psychology, Duke University, Durham NC.

Bryant Stamford, Ph.D., University of Louisville, Louisville KY. Author of *Fitness without Exercise*.

Nancy C. Stevenson, HTR, president of the American Horticultural Therapy Association.

Varro E. Tyler, Ph.D., School of Pharmacy and Pharmacal Sciences, Purdue University, West Lafayette IN. Author of *The Honest Herbal*.

Thomas Wadden, Ph.D., professor of psychology and director at the Center on Health and Behavior, Syracuse University, Syracuse NY.

Hope Weisel, M.S., R.D., St. Luke's\Roosevelt Hospital Center, Weight Control Program, New York NY.

Peter Wood, M.D., D.Sc., professor of medicine, University of California Stanford Center for Research in Disease Prevention, Stanford CA. Author of *The California Diet and Exercise Program*.

I also thank Peter Ciullo of Maradia Press for his advice and consultation; Phil Cornell for his superlative copy-editing; Diana Restuccio for her illustrations and cartoons; John V. Restuccio for his help in securing financing, and, of course, my wife Mabel and two children, Josh and Kristen, for their love and patience while I wrote this book.

Chapter One

A New Approach to Fitness

Fitness the Dynamic Gardening Way: a Health and Wellness Lifestyle introduces a novel approach to gardening. Viewed from a broad perspective, gardening can help you pursue a healthy lifestyle that includes nutritious fruits and vegetables, plenty of exercise, relief from stress, companionship of family and friends, and the aesthetic pleasures of working with nature and the environment.

It encourages a healthy lifestyle you can enjoy for decades—not just another fad diet or exercise program that promises "thinner thighs and a flatter tummy" in a few weeks. While the main goal of gardening may be growing fresh fruits and vegetables, my focus is on the *process* of attaining that goal.

Progress is measured in seasons and years. In fact, I include a *five-year* gardening and exercise plan. The best part is that a natural by-product of your exercise program is bushel baskets full of naturally low-calorie fruits and vegetables.

Contrary to popular opinion, sound nutrition doesn't have to be boring. Home-grown fruits and vegetables offer more variety and taste better than most supermarket produce.

Who should read this book?

❀ It's for anyone interested in health and wellness.

❀ It's for anyone who has tried to lose weight without success.

❀ It's for the thousands of walkers, joggers, and stair-steppers who find their enthusiasm waning and their bellies expanding.

❀ It's for gardeners who want to learn more about fitness.

❀ It's for traditional gardeners who want to learn more about *sustainable* and *intensive* gardening techniques.

❀ It's for avid gardeners who have tried to get their friends and neighbors interested in gardening but haven't been successful.

Dynamic gardening uses *sustainable* and *intensive* gardening techniques. These techniques fall under the broad category known as *organic gardening.* I will further define in Chapter 10 the different types of organic gardening. I use these techniques for three reasons.

First, intensive gardening techniques are more physical than traditional gardening. Double digging raised garden beds is a tough workout. Composting grass clippings and leaves requires energy—calories, and lots of them. Hauling sawdust, cottonseed meal, cotton hulls or common barnyard manure builds arm, leg and back strength.

Second, the organic emphasis on *the soil* creates a longer gardening season than that of traditional gardening. Building a porous, nutrient-rich soil is a year-round activity. Using intensive, raised-bed gardening techniques, you can prepare the soil as early as six to ten weeks before the last frost date.

In the fall and winter, cover-cropping, composting and cutting wood are excellent cardiovascular and muscle-toning exercises. The wide scope of physical activities transforms a seven-month exercise season to a nine-month season.

Third, organic gardening is more of a lifestyle than traditional gardening. Organic gardeners are as concerned about *how* they grow as *what* they grow. They're concerned about environmental issues such as recycling, global warming, ground-water pollution, and the landfill problem.

Don't feel you *have* to adopt strict organic gardening methods to reap the fitness benefits from this book. By strict I mean viewing organic gardening as an all-or-nothing proposition—that you must use *only* organic fertilizers and pesticides. Most organic gardeners stress complete elimination of chemical pesticides and synthetic fertilizers. Eliminating or reducing chemical pesticides and synthetic fertilizers is just a *small part* of the Dynamic Gardening Way to fitness.

Dynamic Gardening is *so much more* than simply an issue of *natural* versus *chemical*. It's about creating a living, healthy soil. Natural resources—grass clippings, leaves and kitchen wastes—are used productively to create compost, the foundation of a successful garden. These resources are no longer wasted in already crowded landfills.

Dynamic Gardening is about working and cooperating with nature. It's about picking strawberries with your children on a sunny, Saturday morning. It's about catching fireflies with your grandchildren at dusk. It's about the sounds of birds chirping at dawn. And, of course, it's about the freshest, best-tasting fruits and vegetables that money cannot buy—at any price.

The ideas and examples proposed in this book will help move you along a continuum, closer and closer, to integrating your health and fitness goals with your gardening lifestyle. Too many gardeners till the soil in early summer, add a quick dash of 10-10-10 fertilizer and head back to the couch. Six weeks later, they find a mass of weeds and wilted vegetable plants for their efforts. Meanwhile, these same frustrated gardeners spend hours each week running, jogging and stair-stepping their way to fitness. Or, even worse, they remain on the couch *thinking* about exercising *tomorrow*.

What's wrong with this picture? Our grandparents did not jog, walk, or stair-step their way to health. They exercised the "old-fashioned way." They gardened. They burned calories while enjoying the garden, saving money, and spending quality time with their families.

If this is such a great idea, then why hasn't gardening ever been proposed before as a comprehensive, lifelong diet and exercise program? Who would promote such an idea? Not the $33 billion weight-loss industry. Not the $1.3 billion weight-loss clinic industry. Not the major food processors and packagers with their "lite" product lines. And definitely not the fast-food franchises found on nearly every street corner.

No, it would have to be the local nurseries and garden centers, the seed companies, organic fertilizer and pesticide firms, tiller and garden-tool companies. Imagine *them* promoting gardening products as part of a comprehensive diet and exercise program. Sounds outrageous, doesn't it?

But it's not. Now the tiller, hoe, and shovel share space with the stair-step machine, treadmill and weight bench. Now, as you count repetitions while doing squats you can plant a rose bush. While you stretch you can weed the flower beds. Between sets of pullups you can cut flowers for your dinner table. Fitness the Dynamic Gardening Way is *the* diet and exercise program for the 90s.

This book is organized by Parts and Chapters:

Part One: Current Diet and Exercise Programs

Chapters 2 and 3 address why existing diet and exercise programs have not been successful in maintaining long-term weight loss. If you've tried any of these diet or exercise programs or are considering using one, please read these chapters first.

If you're already familiar with current diet and exercise programs and want to get straight to the benefits of dynamic gardening, skip to Part 2.

Part Two: Lifestyle

Chapter 4, discusses how traditional exercise programs may advise you to change your lifestyle, but rarely do they *present a health and wellness lifestyle*.

Chapter 5, contrasts the dynamic gardening lifestyle to the traditional diet and exercise programs described in Part One.

Part Three: Exercise

Part three incorporates concepts, techniques and stance from aerobics, weight training and the martial arts. Gardening will be used as a tool to increase endurance, flexibility and strength.

Chapter 6, examines gardening movements in detail and presents a systematic, disciplined approach to gardening to yield maximum aerobic and muscle toning benefits.

Chapter 7, is the Dynamic Gardening Way alternative to working out with weights to build strength and muscle mass: build exercise structures into the landscape of your backyard garden, among the daylilies, daisies and grape vines.

Chapter 8, presents charts showing the muscle groups used during gardening and circuit-training exercises. Use this information to design your own gardening exercise program.

Chapter 9, illustrates the long-term nature of gardening. Other weight-loss programs advertise how quickly you will lose weight. I take the opposite approach. The longer it takes, the better—that's what defines a lifelong health and fitness program.

Part Four: Dynamic Gardening

Part four presents the concepts, techniques and vocabulary of dynamic gardening. This part is for anyone not familiar with gardening and the latest soil-enhancement and space-utilization techniques.

Chapter 10, introduces sustainable and intensive gardening techniques.

Chapter 11, explains the two most important dynamic gardening techniques: how to make compost and prepare intensive, deep-dug, raised garden beds.

Chapter 12, describes in more detail the gardening approach of this book known as Integrated Pest Management (IPM). Chemical and natural fertilizers and pesticides are compared and contrasted.

Chapter 13, presents various ways to start and obtain plants. A virtually fool-proof method of starting plants from seed is introduced.

Chapter 14, presents exercises and gardening activities for each season.

Part Five: Sound Nutrition

Chapter 15, explains why growing your own fresh fruits and vegetables is the best diet alternative to pills, powders and prepackaged meals.

Chapter 16, emphasizes that eating fruits and vegetables is not enough—they must be nutritiously prepared.

Part Six: The Role of the Mind

Chapter 17, examines the psychological components of health and fitness and current theories on eating disorders and weight-loss.

Chapter 18, presents solutions to the many obstacles facing potential gardeners. Whether your concern is frequent travel, poor climate, or simply "not enough time," I offer suggestions on how to overcome obstacles and integrate gardening into your fitness lifestyle.

Chapter 19, explains how careful *attention* to gardening may provide more stress-relief than *trying* to relax.

Chapter 20, presents an overview of successful horticultural therapy programs for individuals with developmental, emotional or physical handicaps, and suggestions on how these techniques can be modified to the general population.

Chapter 21, introduces the psychological technique of visualization, used frequently in professional sports, to help you maintain enthusiasm and achieve your health, physique and gardening goals. Visualization techniques help change your mental image of yourself by replacing "negative self-talk" with positive affirmations.

Chapter 22, introduces business-management techniques to organize your gardening and fitness goals, objectives, strategies, plans and activities.

Part Seven: Children

Chapter 23, presents games and activities to help teach your children how to play and exercise in the garden while growing fresh fruits and vegetables. Involving the entire family is important to the success of the Dynamic Gardening Way fitness program.

Part Eight: Summary

Chapter 24, summarizes *Fitness the Dynamic Gardening Way* with a day in the garden with my family.

Chapter 25, ties all the chapters together into a comprehensive fitness lifestyle.

Part Nine: Appendix

The Appendix includes Sources for supplies, a selected Bibliography, and an Index.

If you're looking for an alternative to traditional diet and exercise programs, *Fitness the Dynamic Gardening Way: a Health and Wellness Lifestyle*, may be the answer for you.

Chapter Two

Why Diets Fail

Every year, about fifty million Americans go on a diet. With great enthusiasm, they drink diet milkshakes, count calories, and fast their way to slimness.

The statistics on diets, however, are not encouraging. Studies show that over *ninety percent* of those who lose weight on a diet program gain the weight back, most within two years. Most doctor-supervised weight-loss clinics see patients who have already failed at one or two diets.

Dr. David Garner, Ph.D., department of psychiatry, Michigan State University and an authority on weight loss, notes, "There is no empirical evidence that any diet can reduce weight permanently for any more than a small percentage of individuals."

Interestingly, every diet book has a chapter on "Why Diets Fail!" Each diet is introduced as the "last diet you'll ever need," yet few break any new ground. Most diet programs stress the need to change eating habits and lifestyle, yet few present a specific health and wellness lifestyle. Many recent popular diet trends have been little more than fads unable to stand the test of time.

Fad Diets

Fad diets typically require a temporary, drastic alteration of your eating habits. They often offer limited nutritional variety and promise greater than two pounds of weight loss per week.

They're popular because they promise quick weight loss, then fall out of favor after the initial enthusiasm wanes. Walk into an average bookstore and look at the titles of current diet books.

The Chocaholics Dream Diet
The Junk Food Diet
Drinking Man's Diet
Beverly Hills Diet
Last Chance Diet

Open any supermarket tabloid and scan the claims for quick weight loss:

"Lose weight while sleeping."
"Eat anything you want and lose weight."
"Lose ten pounds in one week."

Many of these "best-selling" diets share similar characteristics. They promise significant, quick, weight loss requiring little effort on your part. The old adage "if it sounds too good to be true, then it probably is" is especially pertinent to diets. If you put nothing in, you get nothing back.

There is no "secret diet food." Grapefruit doesn't have any magic weight-losing properties. Celery, while very low in calories, doesn't burn calories while you eat it. *Organic* fruits and vegetables, I'm sorry to say, don't have any special "fat-burning" qualities.

One diet, written by a medical doctor, claimed the discovery of a "secret enzyme." There is no such thing as a "magic" or "secret" enzyme, substance or pill. Enzymes are no more than protein. Cooking procedures or hydrochloric acid in the stomach break down all proteins ingested, including purported "fat-burning" enzymes.

Years ago, the "Fat Magnet" pill was claimed to "break into thousands of tiny particles, each acting like a tiny magnet." It supposedly eliminated fat cells from the digestive system as they clung to these particles.

Many popular diets restrict your food intake in one or more ways. A few examples:

Dr. Atkins *High Energy Diet* focuses on reducing carbohydrate intake. This view is contrary to advice from virtually every major health association.

The *Beverly Hills Diet* and *Eat to Win* focus on the combination of foods eaten during a meal. They limit most meals to a single type of food. There is no medical evidence that food combinations have any effect on your ability to gain or lose weight. Since these diets prescribe eating grapefruits and other citrus fruits for several days, quick, short-term weight loss is inevitable.

The *Scarsdale Diet* advocates foods high in protein yet low in carbohydrates and fat. The *Stillman Diet* sold over five million copies using the same idea and the added touch of drinking eight glasses of water a day. Water should be part of every dietary program. However, drinking eight glasses each day is not a secret to losing weight.

The rigid structure, limited variety and nutritional shortcomings imposed by these diets are self-defeating. They are not a long-term strategy for health and wellness.

To lose weight, you must reduce caloric intake below the amount your body needs. Your Basal Metabolic Rate (BMR) is the amount of energy your body needs at rest and not digesting food. The BMR of individuals varies by age, weight and body type. For men, between 1600 and 1800 calories per day is considered average. For women, between 1200 and 1450 calories per day would be average. That is what your body would need per day if you did *nothing* all day long. Your body type, amount of muscle mass and activity level will raise this number considerably higher.

Eating 1,200 to 1,800 calories per day will leave most people with at least a 500 calorie per day deficit. A pound of fat is 3500 calories so this equates to one pound lost per week. Reduced food consumption decreases the likelihood that your vitamin and mineral intake will be sufficient, thereby increasing the impor-tance of eating low-calorie, nutrient-packed foods.

Bad eating habits, however, lead us to fat and sugar-laden junk foods. These empty calories add little nutritional value, further reducing our daily vitamin and mineral intake.

Many dieters supplement their meals with vitamin and mineral pills. Occasionally, supplements may be warranted. However, they are both expensive and lack dietary fiber, an essential ingredient to good health.

Artificial and Short-Term
Most diet-supplement or diet-substitute programs do not take a long-term approach. This is especially true for programs that require pills, powders, and prepackaged meals. Ask yourself:

- ❀ What is the focus of this diet?
- ❀ How does it change my eating habits?
- ❀ How long will I need to stay on this diet?
- ❀ How much will it cost?
- ❀ How does it fit into my lifestyle?

A) Powders

The popular Slimfast™ diet prescribes a Slimfast milkshake for lunch and a sensible meal for dinner. You add the powder to water, fruit juice or milk. Each can costs about five dollars. On this program, you can lose up to two pounds per week.

B) Pills

Pills contain caffeine, fiber, fat emulsifiers, vitamin and mineral supplements and protein. In essence, there's a pill for "what ails ya."

Diet pills contain a variety of substances. Most over-the-counter pills contain caffeine or phenylpropanolamine (PPA), an antihistamine, and benzocaine. While they do reduce your appetite, no one really knows why. They are considered safe, but side effects include headaches, nervousness, rapid pulse, dizziness, sleeplessness, and palpitations. In addition, these pills should not be used by someone with high blood pressure, diabetes, and diseases of the heart, thyroid or kidneys.

The positive publicity for fiber has even created "fiber pills." Besides being an expensive way to obtain fiber, they may give the mistaken impression that you do not need natural fiber from fruits and vegetables.

Doctor-prescribed diet pills contain a variety of stimulants that effectively reduce appetite. However, they may lead to either psychological or physiological dependence, hardly a long-term strategy for health and wellness.

Vitamin supplements are a three billion-a-year industry. Much controversy surrounds a person's need for vitamin supplements. Many experts argue there is little need for vitamin supplements except under specific circumstances—recovering from an illness; for infants; and for pregnant and lactating mothers.

Protein pills are very common among athletes and bodybuilders. Gilbert B. Forbes, M.D., with the University of Rochester Medical School, asserts: "There is no evidence that expensive food supplements do any good." Darrin Brooks, a supervisor of sports medicine and certified athletic trainer with Methodist Hospital in Memphis, Tennessee, states: "All packets and pills provide is expensive urine. Excess nutrients pass through the body."

C) Prepackaged Foods

The medically supervised diets, Nutri-Trim™, Medi-Trim™ and countless others, have been very successful in their marketing of short-term diet success.

Prices vary, but at the writing of this book, losing twenty five pounds at the Diet Center™ costs about $600. The Nutri/System™ plan is about $10 per pound lost, with meals costing from $55 to $65 weekly. You *will* lose weight eating only prepackaged foods. After all, everything you eat and all you eat is in the packet.

Certain people like this type of diet program because it's highly structured and convenient. Prepackaged meals eliminate the need for calorie counting or measuring and ensure they're eating a nutritionally balanced diet.

D) Liquid Protein

The medically supervised diets Optifast™ and Medifast™ are in the category of very-low-calorie (VLC) diets, usually 800 calories a day or less. VLC diets may be warranted for those who are more than fifty pounds overweight and the weight poses a health threat. These diets should always be followed under strict medical supervision.

Based on egg- or milk-protein formulas, these diets are nutritionally balanced. While programs vary, they typically start with a 400 to 800 calorie per day diet for about twelve weeks. A low-calorie meal is added between twelve and sixteen weeks. Losses are dramatic—as high as eleven pounds the first week and three to five pounds per week after that. Costs of VLC diet programs range from $1,200 to $3,000.

Why Diets Fail

There is significant evidence that very-low-calorie diets, under 800 calories per day, work against body physiology. C. Wayne Callaway, M.D., author of the *Callaway Diet* (Bantam), says that one reason diets fail is that "the body adapts to starvation. Studies with animals show that starving leads to binging."

In his book, Dr. Callaway further refutes many diet misconceptions. He explains how the dieting behavior of "Starvers, Stuffers and Skippers" works against the weight-loss results they seek. Based on his years of clinical experience with obese patients, he notes that for many, the reason diets fail is *physiological*—a natural, biologically motivated response to perceived starvation.

Therefore, the very *act* of dieting is what *prevents* you from losing weight. Your body adapts to reduced calories by reducing its metabolic rate, retaining water, and burning calories more efficiently. Consequently, Dr. Callaway advises: "It's important that people set appropriate goals—a healthy weight, versus an ideal or desirable weight."

Research at the University of Pennsylvania has shown that those on medically supervised low-calorie diets regain from one-quarter to two-thirds of their weight within one year. About fifty percent of Optifast™ patients drop out before reaching a "real food" maintenance program. Of those who do remain in the maintenance program, about two-thirds keep off at least one-half their weight loss two years later.

Proponents of these diets note that nutritional counseling and behavioral modification techniques are a major component of their program. Unfortunately, too many patients drop out before completing the maintenance stage. In addition, recent research from G. Kenneth Goodrich and John P. Foreyt at the Baylor College of Medicine assesses the long-term success of these diet programs at about 10 percent. For every one-hundred eager participants, ninety gain most of the weight back.

Diets that eliminate food preparation choices take away personal responsibility. Prepackaged-meals do not change eating habits—they only put them on hold. There is no incentive to change your lifestyle.

Complementary Diet Programs

Several diet programs are complementary with the Dynamic Gardening Way Health and Wellness Lifestyle. The best-selling *T-Factor Diet*, by Dr. George Katahn, focuses on reducing fat grams in your diet. Your body processes fat calories differently than calories from carbohydrate or protein sources. Also, fat, particularly saturated fat found in meat, is a leading cause of heart disease and other ailments. Garden-fresh fruits and vegetables are virtually without fat, yet high in carbohydrates, vitamins and minerals.

The *Callaway Diet* is also complementary with Fitness the Dynamic Gardening Way. Dr. Callaway's revelation that the *process* of dieting is the very reason so many fail, is particularly relevant to the concept of gardening as a fitness program. The best ways to avoid the pitfalls associated with the diet programs mentioned above is eating a sensible diet and exercising regularly. Gardening provides both the exercise and sensible diet.

Susan Olson, Ph.D., clinical psychologist, and author of *Keeping It Off*, notes that:

"Dieters are more successful when they assume ownership of their weight loss. It appears they get into a 'guilt rebellion' mode: when the diet works, they view something *outside themselves* as the healer. In many cases dieters see *the doctor* as the fixer to their weight problem. Yet, when the doctor [or diet] fails, they feel that *they* failed.

"If you [the dieter] do not have ownership, it won't work. I often have to counteract the diet mentality of a clinical diet program. They lose weight for the short term, but they pay a price. The average diet-clinic customer in essence says 'I'm going to be good for a while.'"

Dr. Olson's book, *Keeping it Off*, is different from other weight-loss books. It chronicles the lives of thirty-five successful dieters—those who have lost over fifty pounds and not regained more than five of those pounds within two years. There are no menus, no gimmicks, and no "magic secrets" to success. Her most notable point is that each successful dieter had his or her *own unique system* for losing weight.

Another sensible weight-loss program is Richard Simmons' "Deal a Meal" plan and his emphasis on daily exercise. His program is based on the four major food groups, exercise, and positive reinforcement. Mr. Simmons' premise is similar to mine, that dieting and exercise should be interesting and fun.

Summary

Fad diets and quick weight-loss programs are inherently self-defeating. The majority limit your choice of food in one manner or another. Don't blame yourself for failing to lose weight. Diets work against your inherent biological processes of self-preservation. The greatest flaw of any diet program is the very fact that it *is* a diet program. You're *aware* that you're dieting. Every day you look at the scale to see if you've lost weight, and if the weight loss is not quick and dramatic, you feel as if you've failed.

Another component of being fit is maintaining a consistent exercise program. The next chapter explores the reasons so many have difficulty staying with an exercise program.

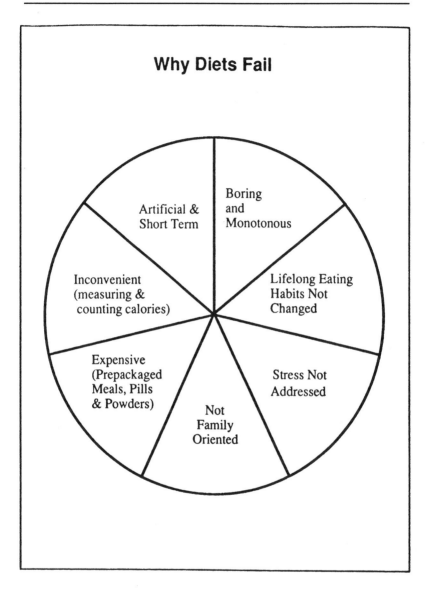

Why Diets Fail

Boring and Monotonous

Lifelong Eating Habits Not Changed

Stress Not Addressed

Not Family Oriented

Expensive (Prepackaged Meals, Pills & Powders)

Inconvenient (measuring & counting calories)

Artificial & Short Term

Chapter Three

Why Exercise Programs Fail

Moderate exercise is universally recognized as a primary component of any well-balanced weight-loss or weight-maintenance program. Aerobics, walking, jogging, swimming and cycling are exercises most often associated with fitness. They all burn calories, improve the cardiovascular system, and build muscle tone. Many people find more fun in competitive team sports: baseball, volleyball, basketball, tennis or soccer.

The problem is typically not *starting* an exercise program; the problem is *staying* with an exercise program. Traditional methods of losing weight—walking on a treadmill or using a stair-step machine—can be boring.

Yes, you can read or watch television while walking on a treadmill. I use one when it's twenty degrees outside and snowing. However, it's definitely more difficult to muster the motivation to walk the treadmill than exercise in the garden. To be successful over the long-term, an exercise program must be enjoyable.

Please don't be misled by the many promises for quick weight loss with little effort. Just as there are fad diets, there are also fad gizmos and gadgets.

Exercise Fads

You're lying in bed and can't sleep, so you press the remote-control's "ON" button for your television. The TV announcer promises that rolling beads will "roll the fat" out of you. Just send $49.95, and it will be shipped to your door.

The marketers of the "Tummy Eliminator," meanwhile, claimed it helped reduce the abdomen. *Consumer Reports* evaluated this device and concluded that while it could tone arms and shoulders, it did virtually nothing to strengthen stomach muscles. *Vibrating belts* shake the stomach a lot but do absolutely nothing to help you lose weight in the thighs or waist. The promoters of *sweat suits* promise weight loss of four or five pounds "while you sleep." The loss is little more than water weight.

These fad gizmos and gadgets should never be mistaken for legitimate exercise equipment. To advertise that weight loss is possible without effort is plain misleading. Simple, old-fashioned pushups and jumping jacks will provide more benefit than wasting money and time on these type of products. However, even legitimate exercise programs fail.

Inconvenient

Dressing for an aerobics class, hiring a baby sitter, driving to the spa, working out, and driving home can be both time-consuming and inconvenient. You may be self-conscious working out in a coed spa. Also, spas are most crowded when you need them most—right after work. I've been a member of a spa for over ten years, and I enjoy working out, but I have never enjoyed waiting on exercise equipment. Perhaps your work schedule doesn't coincide with your exercise program. Some neighborhoods may not be safe in the evening for jogging, walking or cycling.

Requires Expensive Equipment or Health Spa Fees

Exercise equipment costs money. A good treadmill can cost between $500 and $1,500. Good stair-stepping, cross-country skiing and rowing machines cost at least $250 with better quality machines costing more than $500. Exercise equipment costing less than $100 is usually of poor quality and awkward to use.

Health spa fees are easily $20 per month and more. I'm not against purchasing exercise equipment or joining a spa. I've done both. When I travel on business, I go to the spa. During the winter, in addition to gardening preparation exercises, I use exercise equipment in my home. However, if cost has prevented you from continuing with your exercise program, the Dynamic Gardening Way will show you how to keep fit with minimal expense.

Doesn't Include All Members of the Family
Some sports are not family oriented. Golf for example, is seldom enjoyed by the entire family. Jogging, bicycling, rowing, and cross country skiing may not be suitable for young children or elderly people. Some members of the family may not be athletically inclined and prefer noncompetitive activities to competitive team sports.

Not Applicable to Those With Special Physical Requirements
Perhaps your current physical condition does not allow you to enjoy soccer, baseball, tennis and other competitive sports. Sudden start and stop motions—common with handball and tennis—may aggravate knee injuries. People with limited walking ability and confined to a wheelchair are further limited in their choices of interesting and practical exercise programs. Those with sight or hearing impairments may feel uncomfortable exercising in crowded health spas.

Summary
Don't blame yourself for losing interest in a traditional exercise program. Perhaps you cannot find the motivation to continue walking, cycling or stair-stepping every day. Maybe you've lost interest in the local television aerobics program. If you've decided it's time to try something else—you're not alone.

For many, the problem with a specific aerobic or muscle toning program is that it's *just* exercise. While this might sound strange, in the context of exercising while gardening it's an important point. Perhaps you need to change your *lifestyle* to *include* exercise. The next chapter addresses this issue.

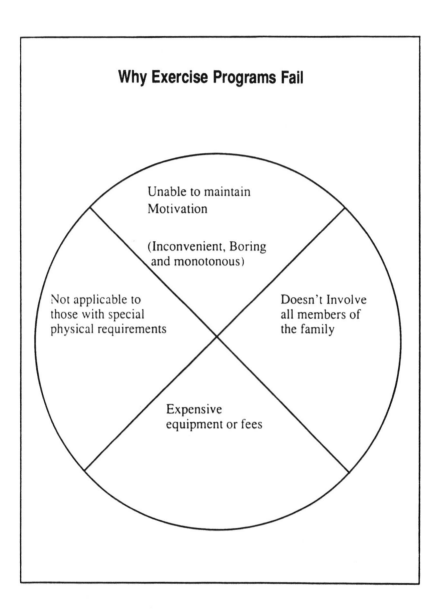

Why Exercise Programs Fail

Unable to maintain Motivation

(Inconvenient, Boring and monotonous)

Not applicable to those with special physical requirements

Doesn't Involve all members of the family

Expensive equipment or fees

Chapter Four

Lifestyle Not Changed

The major drawback of most diet and exercise programs is that they're seldom *integrated*. One moment you're "dieting," the next moment "exercising." Is there a natural flow from one activity to the other? Is there anything that connects your exercise program with the food you eat? Thomas Wadden, Ph.D., professor of psychology at Syracuse University, says: "Dieters need to stop paying attention to weight change and focus more on lifestyle change." A major component of our lifestyle is *what we eat*. One of the main reasons overweight people never lose weight is because they fail to change their eating habits.

Eating Habits Are Not Changed

Your eating habits determine a large part of your ability to maintain or lose weight. The National Cancer Institute recently reported that, on a typical day, forty percent of the American public didn't eat a single portion of fruit and twenty percent not a single portion of vegetables.

Read any magazine article on losing weight, and the experts all give the same advice: Change eating habits. Educators, physicians, nutritionists, and weight-loss support groups across the country stress reducing fat intake, the four main food groups, and low-calorie preparation.

Theories abound on why we *do* eat the wrong foods. For many, eating is a social activity. They eat while visiting with friends or watching a ball game on television or at a bar. Some eat when depressed. Others simply crave sweets: candy, chocolate, cakes and pies.

Many claim they simply "don't like vegetables." Maybe it's because all they can remember are overcooked and over-processed vegetables they ate as a child. Canned, boiled and overcooked vegetables lack taste, texture and nutrition.

I'll never forget the day I harvested fresh asparagus from my garden in early March. A freeze was expected the next day, so I picked a half-dozen spears. My dad was visiting that day. There was only one vegetable he would not eat—asparagus. He never liked the taste and texture of canned asparagus.

We dipped the fresh, raw asparagus stalks in a vinaigrette salad dressing. Dad thoroughly enjoyed the crisp, flavorful asparagus spears. While fresh, store-bought asparagus is certainly better than canned, nothing can beat the quality of fresh-picked.

Integrating Diet and Exercise
While dynamic gardening is the best example of an integrated exercise and diet program, there are others—fishing for example. Sure, you *could* sit on the grass with a bucket of fried chicken and fish (and many do). You could also fish with the explicit *intention* of exercising. You might call it *dynamic* fishing.

Deep-sea fishing, surf fishing, and even genteel, fly fishing require a substantial expenditure of energy. You could add leg and arm weights while fishing from the shore or do jumping jacks and pushups while waiting for the fish to bite. At the very least, while fishing you're not sitting in front of the television set, idly snacking. You're out in the sunshine and fresh air. You're active.

The by-product of fishing is fresh, nutritious fish for the dinner table. Even if the fish aren't biting, you can still enjoy being outdoors. Gardening follows the same pattern with a greater breadth of activities and nutritional benefits.

Summary

The experts—physicians, nutritionists and health associations—advise us to change our lifestyle and eating habits. There is a need for a truly integrated health and wellness lifestyle.

If you've never gardened before, *Fitness the Dynamic Gardening Way* aims to change your lifestyle. Currently, you may drive to the supermarket to purchase produce; go to the spa, gym or tennis courts for exercise; go to a Botanic Garden to enjoy blooming flowers; go to the tanning salon to get a tan; and set aside time to be with your children. In the next chapter I'll show you how to do everything I've just described all *at the same time.*

Take a few moments and write down answers to the following short list of lifestyle questions. It will help you understand how your current diet and exercise program fits into your lifestyle.

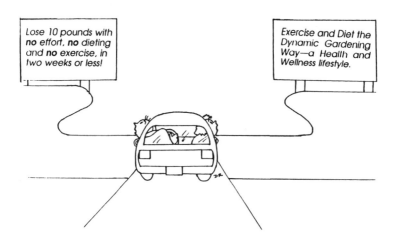

Lifestyle Questions

Health goals: short term_____

Health goals: long term_____

Occupation_____

Hobbies_____

Interests_____

Free time (how important)_____

What's important to you?_____

General health_____

Exercise programs_____

Sports_____

Eating habits_____

Drinking habits_____

Family members (how many) _____

Marital status_____

Creative endeavors_____

Reading (how much)_____

Your local climate_____

Your local geography_____

Food preferences_____

How often do you watch television?_____

How do you spend your leisure time?_____

What do you do on vacations?_____

How often do you travel?_____

How important is convenience?_____

Do you prefer to earn more money?_____

Do you prefer to save more money?_____

Social life_____

Prefer to be alone or with people?_____

Concerned about the environment?_____

Level of stress in your life_____

Value system_____

Spiritual beliefs_____

Chapter Five

The Dynamic Gardening Way

How does the Dynamic Gardening Way differ from other diet and exercise programs? The very fact that it's *not* a diet or exercise program is the secret of its success *as* one. (You've been waiting for the "secret," well, that's it.) Gardening addresses the major reason most diet and exercise programs fail—long-term incentive and motivation. Millions of people garden. Why? Let me count the ways . . . .

Exciting and Fun

About seventy million households garden in America. About thirty million households grow vegetables. One newspaper article recently rated gardening as America's number one pastime.

The reasons why gardeners work the soil vary as much as the plants they grow. They garden to save money. They garden because their parents did. They garden because they love to grow something with their own hands.

Gardening is rewarding because it brings you outdoors, in the sunshine and fresh air. It's exciting to watch a seedling burst from the ground and grow into a plant. It feels good to rake the soil and feel it crumble. It's personally satisfying to eat delicious fresh apples, raspberries and tomatoes you've grown yourself.

Fruits and vegetables are not the only rewards of gardening. Flowers provide a splash of color on a warm summer day. Bushes add structural interest to the garden and a haven for beneficial insects. Trees provide shade for rest after a day exercising in the garden.

The sweet smell of roses, lilies and lavender are the rewards of your labor. Establishing flower beds requires plenty of exercise (note how nothing is "work" once it's part of a comprehensive diet and exercise program.) Not only do garden beds add beauty to your home and neighborhood, each one is worth many pounds in weight loss.

Gardening provides the *positive reinforcement* and *motivation* to maintain an exercise program and eat nutritious fruits and vegetables. Most dieters feel encouraged only when they see dramatic, quick weight loss. What happens when the initial weight loss stops? Most return to their old eating habits and gain the weight back.

Long-Term Focus

Virtually every diet program advertises how *quickly* you will lose weight. There is overwhelming evidence that losing weight quickly is the wrong approach. Recent research has shown that after about twelve weeks of steady weight loss under medically supervised diets, weight stabilizes. Body metabolism adjusts to your new weight, which requires less energy to operate. Also, dieters tend to have a lower metabolic rate than those who don't diet. In other words, your body thinks there is a food shortage and conserves energy by storing it as fat.

This phenomena of eating less but maintaining or gaining weight discourages many dieters. Gardening solves this problem. Even if your weight-loss is negligible you will still enjoy the beauty of your flower garden and the superior taste of home-grown vegetables.

Proponents of diet clinics claim that quick weight loss is what the customers want and they're only providing a needed service.

Perhaps it's time to *change the rules*. Some of the ideas and suggestions in this book might seem strange. Instead of jumping up and down in a spa in trendy leotards, I advise stretching and exercising while you plant, weed, cultivate and harvest fresh produce from your garden.

Gardening is not a short-term fix—it's just the opposite. Unlike the immediate claims of other weight-loss programs, every aspect of dynamic gardening makes you wait—on purpose. The garden will teach you *patience*, which may be the greatest lesson you can learn—and pass on to your children. Focusing on the soil and how you grow plants forces you to develop long-term goals and strategies.

Organic fertilizers are slower-acting than synthetic fertilizers. Many organic pesticides won't immediately kill insect pests but cause them to stop feeding and eventually die. Other techniques, discussed later, beneficial insects, companion planting and interplanting, all take time to perfect and adapt to your particular climate and needs.

As you're digging a hole for an apple tree and joggers stroll past, huffing and puffing, and comment, "that looks like a lot of work," think of the delicious apples you'll be eating in three years. As the power-walkers strut past and shake their heads while you double dig a perennial bed, visualize the coreopsis, daisies, and daylilies that will bloom year after year. And as the cyclist whirls past and scratches his head as you collect leaves, grass clippings and spent plants for the compost pile, think of the tomatoes, peppers and sweet corn you'll be eating in a few, short months. The calories expended today will yield a vibrant, living garden that will nourish you and your family for years to come.

So Inexpensive It Saves Money

Growing fruits and vegetables is not only an inexpensive diet and exercise program, it saves money. You can grow hundreds of plants from a seed packet costing less than a dollar. I've purchased seeds from local pharmacy chains early in the season for as little as ten cents a packet! Several mail-order firms specialize in smaller packets costing twenty-five to fifty cents. The expense of growing high-yield vegetables—tomatoes, peppers, beans, carrots, and peas—is a fraction of their cost at the supermarket.

Limit your initial investment in gardening tools. For most gardeners, all you need is a shovel, rake and hoe. Purchase used tools at flea markets or estate sales.

A garden 600 to 1,000 square feet can easily grow most of the fresh fruits and vegetables for a family of four throughout an extended (three-season) growing period. Families that dry, freeze, and can produce will save even more.

Compost, the primary fertilizer and soil conditioner of the dynamic garden, is produced from waste products: grass clippings, leaves, table scraps and barnyard manure.

Convenient as Your Own Backyard or Community Garden.

Gardening has no set hours. You may start at the crack of dawn and finish whenever you like (see gardening at night in Chapter 18). Fancy leotards or expensive running shoes aren't necessary. Any old clothes will do.

You can grow fresh strawberries, spinach, lettuce and tomatoes—just steps from your kitchen. Community gardens are established in many urban areas. If one doesn't exist in your area, start a community garden and discover the pleasures of gardening with family and friends.

Family Oriented

Gardening is a diet and exercise program the whole family can enjoy, together, cooperating with one another toward a common goal. Children, parents and grandparents can all join in the fun. Gardening is a *social* activity. Being outside, away from the television and other distractions, is conducive to conversation.

Applicable to Those With Special Physical Requirements

Millions of senior citizens garden. Unlike other sports and exercise activities that have to be abandoned as you grow older, gardening can be modified to your particular physical requirements. You need not have speed, strength or size. Poor eye-hand coordination and slow reflexes are just fine.

For senior citizens, gardening offers many rewards. You can tailor the level of activity to their ability to bend and kneel. Philip J. Garry, Ph.D., of the University of New Mexico School of Medicine, notes that, "The elderly have the time; gardening is a great thing to encourage."

Raise garden beds to wheelchair height for those with limited mobility. Use markers in the garden to assist the vision-impaired and plant vegetables, herbs and flowers with strong fragrances—basil, sage, lemon balm, mint and rosemary.

Change Your Eating Habits

The dynamic gardening lifestyle integrates sound nutrition, exercise, and stress reduction into a pleasant leisure activity. The benefits of lowered food costs, increased convenience, and improved taste help to mold and shape your eating habits.

This "diet book" is the first ever to explain *how* to make fruits and vegetables more convenient, fresher, better tasting, and more nutritious. That factor alone differentiates the Dynamic Gardening Way from all other diet and fitness programs. The greatest change in eating habits will occur naturally, as a by-product of your growing efforts. Since you expend time and energy to grow fresh fruits and vegetables, there is more incentive to eat them.

The garden will, in effect, be coaxing you to eat healthier food. During midsummer, when zucchini and tomato plants are at full harvest, you'll not only be eating tomatoes and zucchini every day but so will your friends and co-workers! Abundance is a benefit. Fruits and vegetables will be plentiful, inexpensive and fresh. Share with others whatever you can't eat. The remaining produce goes into the compost pile. Nothing is wasted.

Gardening certainly cannot *prevent* you from eating fattening foods. But it can help. Growing strawberry plants will provide fresh strawberries for dessert. Fresh herbs such as marjoram, thyme, and basil will provide a convenient substitute for salt on your vegetables. The superior taste of home-grown tomatoes, cucumbers, and asparagus will help your transition from the junk-food rack to the garden for your snacks.

When you involve the children in the planting, growing and harvesting of fruits and vegetables, they will be more motivated to taste them. Their personal pride of accomplishment will provide the incentive to eat the beans, carrots or spinach on their plates. After all, they grew the vegetables *themselves*.

Change Your Lifestyle

While other diet and exercise programs boast "lose weight without changing your lifestyle," the goal of *this* book *is* to change your lifestyle. No other lifestyle covers the breadth of proper nutrition and exercise activities as Dynamic Gardening.

Gardening is a lifestyle that includes beautiful crocus bursting through a light snow in late winter, daffodils brightening up an early spring morning, sweet juicy tomatoes adorning a summer salad, and colorful chrysanthemums tempering the onset of fall. A cornucopia of colors, fragrances, and textures that excite the senses and soothe the soul.

Instead of focusing on losing weight, *enjoy the gardening experience*—the sunshine and fresh air, the company of family and friends, freshly cultivated soil, and beautiful flowers, fruits and vegetables.

There is a snowball effect: The more you enjoy gardening, the more time you'll spend in the garden, the more fresh fruits and vegetables you'll produce, and the more calories you'll expend. The more fresh fruits and vegetables you eat, the healthier you'll be. The weight loss will appear effortless because you're not *focused* on it. You gardened. I'm not promising a rose garden, but if you want to, grow one—it's part of your diet and exercise program!

In return for the effort invested, gardening can reward you in so many different ways that virtually everyone can find an aspect that motivates them. Losing five pounds in one week is not only unrealistic, it's a short-term fix, a recipe for failure, not a lifelong solution. To lose weight and maintain muscle tone you must continue, year-in and year-out, with your diet and exercise program.

Whether you love to watch things grow, want to share your harvest with family and friends, or want fresh herbs for your dinner parties, it doesn't matter. All that matters is that it's rewarding enough to continue—for a lifetime.

Your motivation to continue your fitness program will be the thrill of seeing a plant grow from a seed, the taste of fresh sweet corn on a warm summer day and the smiles from your family and neighbors when you share your harvest with them. Few moments compare to the joy in a child's voice when she proclaims, "I grew it myself"; the sparkle in a little boy's eyes when he bites into a fresh, red strawberry; and the warm, relaxing feeling of cultivating the soil on a cool spring day with the sun on your face and the worries of the world behind you.

The Dynamic Gardening Way does not preclude any other diet or exercise program. There is no need to buy additional exercise equipment. However, if you already enjoy sports or an exercise program, view Dynamic Gardening as a *cross-training* program. Just be sure to keep a bowl of fresh strawberries, tomatoes or blueberries placed conveniently in the kitchen. Every time you walk past, you'll automatically reach for fresh, nutritious, natural foods. These are the fruits of your labor. You *walked* while you harvested them, you *lunged* as you weeded, and you *pushed* your lawn mower as you collected grass clippings for the compost pile.

Digging holes, hauling produce, raking and even lowly weeding are now part of a comprehensive exercise regimen. Harvesting the produce is part of your "all you can eat" diet program. "Convenience food" is fresh produce picked from the garden prepared as simply as possible: raw, steamed or baked.

Dynamic gardening as a fitness lifestyle is analogous to a strategic business plan for a corporation. An integrated business plan should include goals and objectives for the *entire* corporation.

In business, departments often attempt to find a solution for a problem that addresses only *their* department without viewing the business as a whole. A solution that addresses the needs of marketing, for example, may not be compatible with the needs of finance or manufacturing. This approach is doomed to failure because of the lack of integration. This is analogous to specific diet or exercise products. They only solve a small part of the fitness equation.

Both business *and* fitness goals should address the needs of the whole, not separate, unconnected parts. Business strategies should include all departments. A fitness strategy should include the physical, nutritional *and* mental components of fitness.

Living Longer and Enjoying It More

In Dr. Dan Georgakas' book, *The Methuselah Factors*, he identifies the lifestyles and secrets of the world's longest living people. He notes the following controllable aspects of lifestyle as highly correlated with a long life:

❀ A diet that includes fresh fruits and vegetables.
❀ Moderate exercise.
❀ Lack of stress.
❀ Enjoyable and continual activity.
❀ Safe environment (pollution, crime, noise).

Most of the people in his book are small scale farmers and gardeners who remain active and healthy well into their nineties and beyond. The elderly citizens living in the Russian village, popularized by the Danon™ yogurt commercials mainly grew their own food.

They shared the following traits:

❀ They gardened at a steady but unrushed pace.

❀ They were physically active all their lives.

❀ They ate mostly fresh fruits and vegetables they grew themselves.

❀ They worked in family units, with friends and neighbors.

❀ They experienced a sense of belonging, sharing their harvest with one another and developing a sense of community.

Does the above description sound familiar? It should. It describes *Fitness the Dynamic Gardening Way*.

Summary

The Dynamic Gardening Way is a fitness lifestyle. When compared with the hundreds of popular diet and exercise programs available today, its comprehensive and long-range focus stands apart.

I propose growing your own food and spending your hard-earned money on gardening tools and supplies that will last a lifetime. Whether you want "thin thighs and a flatter tummy," "broader shoulders and powerful pecs," or a comfortable, healthy weight for your body type, the Dynamic Gardening Way can help. It's a fitness program that's most successful when you're not focused on losing weight but exercising while growing fresh fruits and vegetables.

The next chapter introduces the exercise component of the Dynamic Gardening Way.

Chapter Six

The Exercise Program

The typical impression of gardening is that it's a good way to relax, enjoy the outdoors and grow fresh vegetables. Gardening is seldom recommended as an exercise program. The Dynamic Gardening Way Exercise Program aims to change this perception.

Techniques from several disciplines will be added to gardening movements: stretching and stance from the martial arts, repetition and movement from aerobic conditioning, and resistance principles from weight-training. The Dynamic Gardening Way Circuit Training Program adds traditional exercises: pullups, push-ups and sit-ups to exercise the chest, arms and stomach muscles. This mix covers the entire range of exertion—from heart-pumping, muscle-straining, sweat-dripping double digging, to leisurely stretching and toning while cultivating and weeding.

Anyone starting an exercise program *should first consult a physician.* Yes, you might get some strange looks, but exercising the Dynamic Gardening Way can be strenuous. While you're at the doctor's office, please show him this book. I've learned from my interviews that gardening is popular with doctors, however most of them have never thought of it as a comprehensive fitness lifestyle. Using the techniques in this chapter, gardening can now be included with jogging, walking, swimming and other good aerobic exercises.

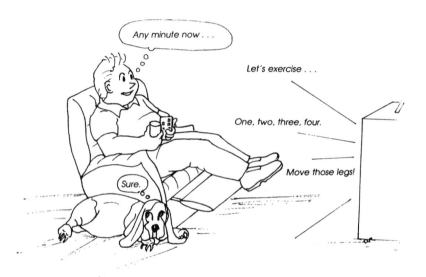

Expending calories and toning muscles are not the only benefits from gardening. Dr. Peter Wood, Ph.D., professor of medicine at Stanford University, and author of *The California Diet and Exercise Program*, notes "Gardening would be good for people not into competitive sports. Schools tend to view exercise as being either on or off the team. Either you're on the basketball team or you sit in the stands and cheer." With gardening, everyone can not *only* cheer but get involved.

Jeffrey Blumberg, Ph.D., professor of nutrition, Tufts University, says that "Gardening may offer more of a reward and more positive reinforcement than other exercise activities to many people. A healthy diet and lifestyle can reduce the risk for diseases associated with diet. It is important to stress 'health span' over 'life span.'"

David Garner, Ph.D., a psychologist at Michigan State University specializing in weight-loss research, advises: "Emphasize the health benefits of gardening and that moderate exercise has been shown to reduce mortality rates." Therefore, even moderately strenuous gardening, properly done, will provide health benefits. Don't feel you have to "go for the burn" each time you garden. Be conscious of your movements, and work at a steady but unhurried pace.

Most gardening is done in the morning. Research has shown that raising the pulse rate at least twenty minutes in the morning will raise metabolism for several hours thereafter. Light gardening exercises, mulching, cultivating, and harvesting, done half an hour before eating or about forty minutes after eating, can burn extra calories.

For those trying to change their figure or physique, strict dieting is probably the worst strategy when working against genetic or body-type factors. Dr. Callaway asserts "About fifty percent of our adult weight is due to heredity." Exercise will be more successful in transforming your body type and increasing basal metabolic rate.

Therefore, for some, the "thin thighs and flat stomach" you so ardently desire may not be within your genetic makeup. A thin, sleek figure or physique may work against your body type. *Some* change is possible with a comprehensive exercise and bodybuilding regimen. It all depends on your level of motivation and the time and energy you put into your exercise program.

The fact that gardening can be enjoyed so many ways is a plus for anyone who wants to change his or her body type but has been unable to do so. If your goal is strength, endurance and low body weight, spend an extra half-hour each day digging garden beds, weeding or doing push-ups between weeding exercises.

Figure 6.1 Awkward stance—a sore back in progress.

Leg Stance

Many gardeners bend over from the waist and use their *backs* to dig, weed, hoe and cultivate, rather than their *legs*, the body's largest muscles. The result is back strain.

Whether you're reaching down, picking something up or moving a shovel full of dirt, the technique is the same. Use your legs.

Figure 6.2 Correct "Stance" using hoe with handle.

Lower your entire body to the ground by stretching, kneeling, squatting or sitting. When you use a hoe, rake or shovel, move toward the ground by bending at the knees. If you're tall, always purchase long-handled tools. Four-foot handles are just too short for a person taller than six feet. Exercising your legs while gardening is equivalent to stair-stepping, walking, and cycling.

When turning compost, bend at the knees with both legs. Fill the shovel with compost and raise your body using your legs to move the compost from one bin to another.

If you ever find yourself bending at the waist to pick something up, stop! Be aware of all that you do in the garden. Carry a piece of paper with you and take notes. Tie a string around your finger. Use a wrist counter and count how often you bend using your back. Place fluorescent orange markers in the garden as a reminder to straighten your back and use your legs.

Practice your leg exercises away from the garden. When you travel, do the leg bending movements listed in this chapter in your hotel room for about thirty minutes.

If you have difficulty bending your knees, either stand while gardening or raise your garden beds to waist level so you can plant and cultivate while sitting. Garden carts, pads and kneelers are available from the garden supply companies listed in the Appendix.

Repetitions and Sets

Group raking, hoeing and cultivating exercise motions into "sets" of twelve to fifteen repetitions. Rest after each set for thirty to sixty seconds, then continue with another until you've completed three to four sets.

Your particular fitness goal will decide the number of repetitions and sets for each exercise. For maximum caloric expenditure, endurance, muscle-toning and "definition," perform fifteen to twenty repetitions in sets of three or four.

Definition, in bodybuilding terminology, is the sculpting of the body for optimal exposure of muscularity. You achieve definition by using a high number of repetitions and reducing body fat to a minimal level.

You build muscle mass by performing fewer repetitions with greater weight or resistance. Weight lifters simply add more pounds to the barbell. You achieve greater muscle mass the Dynamic Gardening Way with a little ingenuity, plenty of determination, and some old-fashioned exercises.

Turning compost, double digging and digging holes are the most strenuous gardening exercises. Circuit Training structures, described in the next chapter, add pullups, chest dips, and sit-ups to round out your gardening fitness program.

Hand Grip

You dig, rake or hoe with either a right- or left-handed grip. Each grip uses a different set of muscles. Alternate your grip after each set of repetitions to balance the muscle groups used. If you're right-handed, rake or hoe first with a right-handed grip, then switch to a left-handed grip.

At first, this will feel awkward. It will take weeks and months to adjust to using a new set of muscles. However, after practice, alternating your grip will become automatic, an unconscious action as you transform gardening movements into an exercise program.

Duration

If you're like most gardeners, you'll garden as long as it takes to get the job done. For optimal health benefits, gardening should be broken into two and three hour periods rather than marathon sessions of six and ten hours. Also, space out activity during the week. Workouts should ideally be at least every other day. It's important to allow at least thirty minutes a few times a week for each garden workout. A thirty minute workout should be brisk, with a conscious effort to warm-up, increase your heart rate and properly cool down afterward.

Gardening activities are so varied and the environment so pleasant that you will typically garden for more than thirty minutes. I rarely garden less than two hours at a time. Exercising for longer periods of time burns the same amount of calories as more intense but shorter-duration activities.

Bryant Stamford, Ph.D., an exercise physiologist at the University of Louisville and author of *Fitness Without Exercise,* adds: "Instead of doing five hours Saturday and doing nothing during the week, it would be best to divide gardening activity during the week the same as you would any other physical activity."

Need for Exercise

Before you start, take a few moments and write down your exercise and fitness goals. Setting goals and objectives is discussed in more detail in Chapter 22. If you've been inactive and you're a novice gardener, start a small garden—just one or two 4' x 8' beds. I cannot emphasize this enough. You should always enjoy exercising in the garden. If you find yourself mumbling and grumbling about "all this garden w—k" when you'd rather be fishing then it's time to reassess your gardening and fitness objectives.

If you already exercise more than seven hours a week, view gardening exercises as a cross-training program. Use weeding to stretch leg muscles. Turn the compost to strengthen arms and legs. Use the perennial flower bed as a focal point for rest and relaxation. Focus on the nutritional and psychological benefits of gardening.

Exercise Without Conscious Effort

You may be thinking, "Concentrating on repetitions and sets and hand grips and exercising is going to take all the fun out of gardening!" That won't be the case.

At first, any new endeavor will take conscious thought. When you first rode a bicycle you thought about it—and probably fell often. When you first learned to play a musical instrument you had to think about the notes before you played them. A dancer learns a series of movements and practices them over and over again. Once the basics are mastered you ride the bicycle without effort, you play music not notes, and you dance with grace and feeling. After practicing the movements I've prescribed in this book, you will eventually do them without thinking. It will just happen. At that point you'll have integrated your exercise program into your gardening lifestyle.

The Exercise Program

As an exercise program, gardening assumes the same pattern of stretching, warm-up, exertion and cool-down as an aerobic exercise class. The main difference is that you'll be exercising in your back yard or community garden instead of the spa.

Always drink plenty of *water* both during and after all gardening exercise. Plants need water, and so do you. It is best to drink water before gardening. Don't wait until you're thirsty. Perspiring heavily also depletes potassium, which can be replenished by eating potassium-rich soybeans, lima beans, rice bran and bananas.

Stretching

It's important to stretch and warm-up your muscles before gardening. Don't overexert yourself the first couple of days if you've been inactive most of the winter. Stretch both before and after gardening.

Charlie Norelli, M.D., from Good Shepherd Rehabilitation Hospital in Allentown, Pennsylvania, says: "You would not do high hurdles without first stretching and warming up. However, many gardeners work in the yard without proper stretching and warming up."

This is so true. Improper preparation can easily ruin the gardening experience. Dr. Norelli adds: "If you are out of shape, you have a high likelihood of straining your back and other areas unless you learn proper body mechanics through a specific flexibility program."

Darrin Brooks, M.S., a certified athletic trainer, and supervisor of sports medicine at Methodist Hospital in Memphis, Tennessee, adds an interesting insight: "One of the reasons gardeners injure their backs or become sore so often is that, typically, gardeners are on their own in terms of execution, whereas team sports are taught in a very disciplined way. Therefore, a lot of gardeners bend and exercise improperly."

Gordon Cummings, Second Dan and a martial arts instructor in Cordova, Tennessee, adds:

"Stretching is an inherent instinct we often ignore. Have you ever watched a dog or cat after they get up from being dormant for a period of time? What is the first thing they do? They stretch! They stretch every muscle they have. It's an instinct. Humans have that same instinct when we get up in the morning; we stretch our arms, but leave it there. It doesn't take a lot of time, but too often we just don't take the time we need to fully stretch every muscle.

"Think of your muscles in terms of concrete. As long as you keep it moving, concrete is soft, but once you let it set—it hardens! Muscles are the same. Stretch your muscles and stretch your life span!"

Stretching Program

Dress in comfortable, loose clothing. Breathe in and out deeply several times. Stand straight, with arms stretched out in front of you, bend at the waist, and touch the ground. Hold your legs straight. Stretch thoroughly, moving your hands first to your right foot and then to your left foot. Slightly bend your knees and repeat the motion. Straighten your legs and spread them out to the sides a little more. Pay attention to your breathing as you stretch. As you stretch, breathe out. Relax. Breathe in and stretch a little further as you breathe out. Repeat this sequence of motions several times.

Stand straight with your legs bent slightly at the knee. Hold a broom handle or rake over your head. Bend at the waist and twist your body first toward your left foot and then toward your right foot. Hold the broom handle over your head and standing straight, twist your torso side to side a dozen times.

Figure 6.3 Hold a rake or broom handle over your head.

Figure 6.4 Bend to the right and then the left.

While standing, spread your legs out to the side. Turn to the left, and slide down into an American-split position below. Stretch your hands forward, and touch your left foot. Raise your body with your hands and reverse your position to your right side. Stretch and touch your right foot. Breathe out as you stretch. Continue to stretch and switch sides.

Figure 6.5 "American Splits"

Spread your legs wide and sit down. In martial arts this is known as a "Korean split." Stretch your hands forward and down to the ground. Move your legs out as far as they will go, breathe out and first touch your left foot and then your right foot. Repeat this motion.

Figure 6.6 "Korean Splits"

Standing straight, spread your legs to the side about two feet. Keep your legs straight. Touch the ground with your hands. Bend your legs at the knee, and continue to stretch and touch the ground. With your hands on the ground, straighten your legs. Spread your legs to the side a little more and continue.

Continue to breathe, stretch and relax your entire body:

✿ With hands on your waist, twirl your hips in a circular motion.
✿ Roll your head around your shoulders to the left, then to the right.
✿ Twirl your arms in windmill fashion.
✿ If a chin-up bar is available, grasp the bar and hang to stretch and loosen muscles.
✿ Walk around the garden and pay attention to your muscles. Arch your back and reach up. Bend over and touch your toes.

Lunge and Weed
Combine stretching with light gardening exercises. Stand before a garden bed and step forward with your left leg, bending the knee as far down as you can, keeping your right leg straight behind you with the knee almost touching the ground. Weed or cultivate with a hand tool for about ten seconds. Stand up and continue alternating legs. Continue lunging, stretching and weeding until you feel well stretched (or you've weeded all the beds).

Figure 6.7 Lunge and Weed

Warmup

After stretching, start with light aerobic exercises: inspecting, weeding, cultivating and mulching. Maintain a steady rhythm from one activity to another.

Inspecting and Spraying

Periodically inspect plants for disease or insect pests. Some insect pests, such as the tomato hornworm, are easily picked off plants and disposed of. Diseased plants should only be added to the compost if you have a "hot" compost pile. If you're not sure, burn or throw away diseased plants.

Occasionally, vegetables or fruit trees need to be sprayed with organic pesticides. Walk briskly while spraying. Add leg weights to increase resistance.

Weeding

Weeding is now a pleasant, twenty to thirty minute aerobic exercise for arms and legs. Always bend at the knees, never the waist.

While hand weeding, spread your legs and bend at the knees. Weed for about twenty seconds. Still in the wide stance, straighten your legs. Spread them out wide, bend your knees and continue weeding. Continue with this sequence. It will take time for this to feel comfortable.

As illustrated in Figure 6.9, set one knee down behind you, your other leg in front of you, knee bent, foot on the ground. Weed for about twenty seconds. Stand up and alternate legs. You may want to carry a foam garden mat to place under your knee.

Figure 6.8 Weeding bed using a wide, knees-bent stance.

Figure 6.9 Weeding bed on one knee, using leg weights.

Squat with your feet flat on the ground, bending at both knees, and your elbows resting on the inside of your legs. Weed for about twenty seconds, stand up and repeat. You may not be able to do this until you've gained a degree of flexibility. Keep at it. It will take months of stretching every day to increase and maintain flexibility.

Figure 6.10 Squatting down with both legs and weeding.

Figure 6.11 Weeding with both knees down.

You can alternate between six weeding positions:

1) Standing straight using "The Stance." (Figure 6.2)
2) Lunge and weed.(Figure 6.7)
3) One foot flat on ground, one knee bent (Figure 6.9).
4) Squatting with both legs (Figure 6.10).
5) Both knees down (Figure 6.11).
6) Sitting and weeding (not illustrated).

If bending on one or both knees is uncomfortable, sit and weed or stand straight using a long-handled weeder such as an "action hoe." For maximum aerobic benefit, maintain a steady rhythm and alternate your grip. Don't worry about what the neighbors say. Gardening exercise may look funny, but health and wellness is a serious matter.

Mulching
Use a wheel barrow or garden cart. Lift the wheel barrow with your legs, back straight. If you mulch with a basket, always squat, feet flat (if you can) when picking it up. As you spread the mulch around your plants, lower your body with your legs.

Exercise Section

Cultivating
Whether you use a hoe, rake, or mini-tiller, the technique is the same:

❀ Keep your back straight.
❀ Spread out your legs in a wide, knee-bent stance.
❀ Alternate your grip.
❀ Think in terms of sets and repetitions (it's not necessary to count actual numbers).
❀ Breathe in and out in a steady rhythm.

Adding a grip to the handle improves leverage.

Power Building Exercises

Posthole Digger
Use a posthole digger to spot-dig deep holes in your garden and exercise chest, shoulders and trapezius muscle groups. It is effective for digging two foot holes for perennials, small bushes and root crops.

Figure 6.12 Using a posthole digger.

Digging and Turning Compost

Digging, double digging and turning compost will build strength and endurance. These exercises will be explained in greater detail in Chapter 11. All beginners should approach these activities cautiously. Stretch thoroughly, maintain a steady pace and be careful not to overexert yourself. Be aware of the natural tendency to bend from the waist while digging. Spread your legs, bend at the knees and use your legs and arms to raise the shovel. Using your legs also burns the most calories.

Circuit Training

If you want a harder workout, build the Circuit Training exercise structures for pull-ups, dips and situps described in the next chapter.

Cool Down, Have a Drink (of your favorite beverage) and Enjoy

Harvest your fruits and vegetables. Walk around the garden at a leisurely pace. Rest, have a drink and enjoy the flowers, butterflies, birds, and other sights and sounds of the garden.

Fall and Winter Exercises

As the harvest winds down and the cold weather looms, do not despair. Dynamic Gardening Way exercises don't stop during the winter.

When the outside temperature is above freezing, bundle up and turn the compost pile for thirty minutes once a week. Another good activity is double digging small sections of the garden. Fill the holes with compost, decayed leaves or topsoil.

Starting, repotting and transplanting plants provides activity, even if it's not particularly strenuous. The activity serves well to keep your mind occupied and your body off the couch and out of the refrigerator.

Construction Projects

Building cold frames, soil sifters, and potting benches is a good way to keep active during the winter and create a useful gardening tool. The magazines and books referenced in the Appendix offer dozens of weekend projects that will add immeasurably to your gardening efficiency, effectiveness and enjoyment.

Cutting Wood

Cutting wood was one of former President Reagan's favorite exercise and relaxation activities. When splitting a log be sure to set it on a log or other support *at your waist level.* You should not have to bend your back as the ax head splits the log. Cutting wood is an excellent example of how one activity yields many benefits. It warms you *six times.*

1) Sawing or chopping down a tree is a vigorous aerobic activity exercising arms, chest and back.

2) Splitting wood exercises the arms, chest, latissimus dorsi, and back.

3) Hauling and stacking wood exercises the legs and lower back.

4) Burning wood heats the home while reducing energy bills and the need for other fuel sources.

5) The aesthetic value of a warm fireplace on a cold winter night, combined with a fitter you, a bottle of wine, and your special someone, may just do wonders for your social life. (See, the Dynamic Gardening Way can impact *every* part of your life!)

6) Wood ashes are an excellent organic fertilizer. Save the ashes in a metal can or bag. Apply them to the garden immediately before preparing the garden beds in the spring. Rain leaches pot ash (potassium) out of the soil. Therefore, apply it at the last possible moment before planting.

Cutting wood—an excellent example of the integrated focus of dynamic gardening as a lifelong health and wellness program.

Cross-Training Exercises

Continue or add cross-training exercises during the winter months. Ice skating, cross-country skiing, basketball, Akido, and aerobic classes can help fill in the gap between the very coldest months and the first spring thaw.

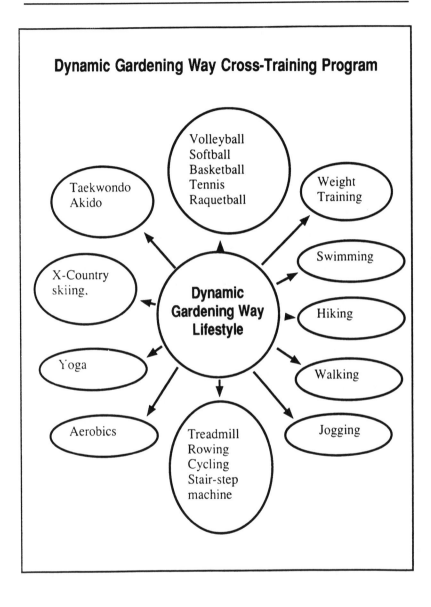

Dynamic Gardening Way Cross-Training Program

Volleyball
Softball
Basketball
Tennis
Raquetball

Taekwondo
Akido

Weight
Training

X-Country
skiing.

**Dynamic
Gardening Way
Lifestyle**

Swimming

Hiking

Yoga

Walking

Aerobics

Treadmill
Rowing
Cycling
Stair-step
machine

Jogging

Gardening & Competitive Sports

For some, gardening will be a cross-training activity to their primary exercise program or sport. Gardening can also serve as an *alternative* to competitive sports.

Golfers are always reminded of their mistakes as they slice into the sand trap. Tennis, handball, softball and basketball are highly competitive. Basketball teams compete for hours to have a score decided by one point and one team goes home a loser.

I don't have anything against competition; it's what made America great. Competition in sports, with the proper perspective, builds character, raises the level of play and provides great entertainment. However, for many, competition does not motivate them. It only adds excess stress and pressure. You may not have the speed, strength, size or endurance for competitive sports.

Gardening is noteworthy because it's not competitive—unless you're attempting to grow a world-record pumpkin. The idea that *large* vegetables are prize-worthy, is outdated. The emphasis should be on the quality of the vegetables and methods used to grow them, not sheer mass. There is no nutritional or health benefit to growing large vegetables. Younger and smaller vegetables taste best. Gardening is an activity where, for once, smaller, slower and gentler become desired traits.

Gardening is an alternative for those who prefer to compete against themselves and the vagaries of nature. It is ideal for those who seek more qualitative and spiritual rewards from their lifestyle. It doesn't have any inherent cultural or sexual bias. Gardening is truly an activity for everyone, in which young and old, rich and poor, quick and slow, big and small can be on the same playing field.

I don't know which has been more enjoyable, eating fresh sweet corn, taking a nap after a few hours exercising in the garden, or catching fireflies at dusk with my children. It doesn't really matter. I felt good during the activity and I felt good after.

Summary

Exercising the Dynamic Gardening Way is comparable to going to the spa, except that before you leave, you're handed a basket full of juicy strawberries every time; power-walking to the supermarket and receiving a ninety-percent discount on fresh tomatoes before you leave; or cycling twelve miles and coming home to a fresh spinach salad after each workout.

The techniques and concepts presented in this book refine the gardening process to achieve optimal flexibility, aerobic and muscle-toning benefits. Adopt the ones you like and don't be afraid to invent your own.

Just remember:

❀ Stretch thoroughly, both before and after gardening.

❀ Use visual cues to remind yourself to breathe in and out, stretch and relax your body as you exercise and garden.

❀ Warm-up, exercise and cool down just as you would any other aerobic exercise.

❀ Use your legs, not your back!

❀ Use the positions that are comfortable for you and try others as your body becomes flexible and limber.

❀ Space out workouts in the garden at least every other day or alternate with other exercise activities.

❀ Have fun exercising in the garden.

Chapter Seven

Circuit Training

Gardening activities—digging, cultivating and planting—are skewed toward leg, arm and back muscle groups. Some exercise motions are not typical gardening movements—pulling your hand to your shoulder, pulling down from above, and pulling your legs to your body (as in a "crunch" sit-up). Circuit Training exercises complement gardening exercises to further build muscle mass and round out muscle groups. Adding a chinup/pullup bar, a sit-up board, and other structures provides additional exercise for biceps, triceps, latissimus dorsi, and stomach muscles.

Chinup Bar/ Pullup Bar on Grape Arbor

Add a chinup bar, a length of three-quarter-inch plumbing pipe painted with rust resistant enamel, to an existing grape arbor. If you don't have an arbor, you can build one in about two weekends.

The concept of a combined grape arbor and exercise station is yet another good example of the integrated nature of *Fitness the Dynamic Gardening Way*. Building the arbor expends calories. Growing grapes up the arbor will provide a structural focal point in the garden. After a few short years, the vines will yield delicious, fresh grapes for snacking, canning or dessert. You can use grape leaves in Greek cooking. The arbor will provide an area to plant a variety of shade-loving perennials. Finally, it's a spot to rest under and enjoy the garden.

Figure 7.1 Pullups on Grape Arbor

Pullups are a function of body weight, therefore providing a good measure of your general fitness level. An average goal for men would be three sets of eight pullups. For women, two to five repetitions would be considered good.

If one pullup is too difficult, try this. Build a two-foot high sitting rail around the arbor. Stand on the rail, grab the bar, lean back and do pullups using your legs to help. Practice doing six to eight repetitions this way. You'll exercise your forearms, triceps, biceps, latissimus dorsi and legs.

If you can do more than fifteen pullups and want greater resistance, add ten to twenty-five pound barbell weights, strapped to a weight belt, around your waist. Lower the number of repetitions to between five and eight to build muscle size and strength.

Dip-Bar

The dip-bar is not as common as a chinup bar. Found in most gyms, it provides exercise for the chest, triceps and upper deltoids. The dip-bar is two parallel bars facing toward you that you grab with both hands, arms bent. Raise yourself by straightening your arms. Lower yourself between the bars with your arms by bending at the elbow.

A good goal for men is three sets of twelve dips. For women, three sets of three to five repetitions would be good. Again, if you can't do one, set a box under your legs, and balance resistance between your arms and legs.

Sit-up Board

You can use a sit-up board set at an incline on a box to exercise stomach muscles. Of course, you can do sit-ups in the grass, but an incline board offers more resistance and requires fewer repetitions. You can construct a sit-up board from plywood or two 2' x 12" planks. Fasten an elastic strap or a wood T-bar at the opposite end to hook your feet under.

Figure 7.2 Dip bar.

Figure 7.3 Sit-up board on incline.

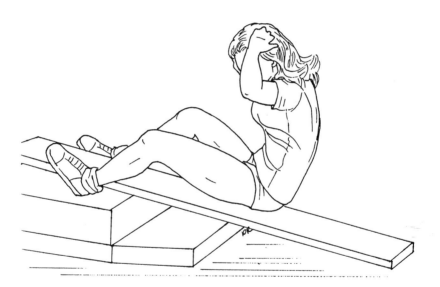

Use Hand Weights, Dumbbells or Milk Jugs.

I call this weight lifting on a budget. If you don't have hand weights available, you can use old plastic milk jugs, filled with water, to exercise the upper deltoids, arms and back. Hold the milk jugs in front of your body and raise up in front of you to shoulder height. Repeat this motion. After two or three sets of twelve repetitions, hold the milk jugs at your side and raise them from your waist laterally out to shoulder height. Each position affects slightly different muscle groups.

Set Up a Box in the Garden

Either build or purchase an old wood box as a step-up box. Weatherproof it, and set it up along an often traveled path in the garden. Every time you walk past, step up and down ten times with each leg. Hold the milk jugs, as in the illustration below, out to the side while stepping up on a box to increase resistance and further tone arms and legs. For an even better aerobic workout, set up several boxes in the garden.

Figure 7.4 Step-up box (log) while holding milk jugs.

Pushups

Ordinary pushups are excellent for building pectoral, triceps and deltoid muscle groups. Try alternating dips and pushups for a complete chest workout. Another option is to do pushups using hand grips attached to a board. They're available in exercise equipment stores. Seeing the pushup grips in the garden will remind you that it's time to "get down and do twenty-five."

If you need more resistance—and have a strong back—have your son or grandson sit on your back while doing pushups. Again, just another way to both involve and enjoy the children while exercising in the garden.

Figure 7.5 Pushups with child (for added resistance).

Roman Chair

This exercise structure is found at most health spas to strengthen stomach and lower back. It's a backless chair with a bar you can hook your feet under. To strengthen stomach muscles, sit on the chair, place your feet under the bar, and bend backward toward the ground and raise up about a dozen times. To strengthen your lower back muscles, lay on the seat facing down, hook your feet under the bar and lower your body to the ground and raise up.

Figure 7.6 Roman chair

Set Up a Pulley On The Grape Arbor

Fasten a pulley to the arbor opposite the chinup bar. Connect a rope to a metal bucket filled with sand or rocks. Attach a bar to the other end for triceps extensions or pull-downs.

Hang a Rope From a Tree

When I was in high school, I always enjoyed climbing a rope to the top of a tree and touching a limb. If your yard has a tree large enough, hang a rope from a good, sturdy branch. If necessary, tie knots every three or four feet. At the end of your gardening workout, climb up and down the rope two or three times.

Ankle Weights/Wrist Weights

To increase resistance and caloric expenditure of all the exercises listed in this book, add ankle and wrist weights while gardening. The added weight will increase the aerobic and muscle-toning benefits of even the simplest gardening movements.

Mini-Trampoline

Use a mini-trampoline to add flexibility and jumping exercises with least impact on joints and tendons.

Commercial Kits

Several commercial jungle-gym kits for children are listed in the Appendix. They can add fun and play to your gardening exercise program with children. They could also be modified for adult use.

Invent Your Own

Set up an obstacle course using old tires. Hang an old tire from a tree, and practice throwing a football through it. Set up a soccer goal, and kick goals between weeding beds. Ideas for exercising in your garden are limited only by your imagination.

Summary

Circuit Training complements and balances the natural exercises of gardening. Whatever your fitness goal, the dynamic gardening lifestyle can help you achieve it. The next two tables suggest sample gardening workouts.

Sample Exercise and Gardening Program

Total weekly workout: 3 hours 20 minutes per week.

Average calories expended are conservatively calculated at five calories per minute. Preparing raised beds, digging, turning compost and Circuit Training exercises will burn approximately ten calories per minute.

(A) Thirty minute workout uses a balanced approach. Short, four minute intervals include a variety of stretching, warm-up, exercise and cool down activities to provide a moderate gardening workout.

(B) Forty minute workout has less variety and longer intervals. Emphasis is on cultivating and planting—ideal for early spring exercise.

(C) Thirty minute workout features turning the compost pile for fifteen minutes as main aerobic and muscle toning component.

(D) Forty minutes of double digging and two Circuit Training exercises, pullups and sit-ups, provide a balanced, aerobic and muscle-toning workout.

(E) Sixty minute, weekend workout features mowing the lawn and a balance between gardening and Circuit Training exercises.

There are hundreds of exercise combinations you can use. Use this as an example to tailor a *Dynamic Gardening Way* exercise program to suite your individual needs.

Sample Exercise and Gardening Program

	(A)	(B)	(C)	(D)	(E)
Calories Expended:	150	200	150	200	300
Duration	30 min	40 min	30 min	40 min	60 min
Stretching	4	5	4	10	4
Removing pests					
Planting	4	10			
Pruning					
Weeding	4	5	3		
Mulching	4	5		5	
Cultivating	4	10	4		6
Double digging				10	
Preparing hole					
Tilling					
Turning compost			15		
Pullups	3			5	5
Dips					5
Sit-ups	3			5	5
Step-up box					
Mowing lawn					30
Harvesting	4	5	4		5
Picking flowers				5	
Walking and enjoying					
Total minutes:	30	40	30	40	60

Workout Suggestions

Five Day:	Mon	Wed	Thu	Sat	Sun
Five Day:	Mon	Tue	Wed	Thu	Sat
Three Day:		Wed		Sat	Sun

Weekend/Holiday Exercise and Gardening Workouts

A) Garden preparation workout program. Emphasis is on gardening exercises. One-hour duration is convenient for early morning (before work), late afternoon (after work), or weekends.

B) Balanced two-and-a-half hour workout covers full breadth of gardening exercises. Illustrates how spending a little time on each activity adds up.

C) Focused three-hour workout splits between fundamental gardening activities: planting, weeding and cultivating, and Circuit Training (fifty minutes).

D) Three-hour mid-season weekend workout. Assumes beds are prepared. This workout includes twenty minutes warming up, thirty minutes on garden maintenance, twenty minutes turning the compost pile, sixteen minutes Circuit Training, sixty minutes mowing the lawn and twenty-six minutes cooling down and enjoying the garden.

E) Long, three-and-a-half hour program focuses entirely on gardening exercises for workout. This program is typical of early spring workouts, when planting and bed-preparation activities are greatest. Note that calories expended, at a very conservative 300 per hour, are over 1000. A more likely estimate is 1200 to 1800—a great way to build a hearty appetite!

Weekend/Holiday Exercise and Gardening Workouts

1 to 3½ hours each

Workout	A	B	C	D	E
Approx. Calories Expended:	300	750	900	900	1050
Duration in hours	1	2.5	3	3	3.5
	-----	-----	-----	-----	-----
Stretching	5	5	5	10	10
Removing pests		5		5	
Planting	5	10	15		30
Pruning		5		5	
Weeding	5	10	15	10	20
Mulching	5	5		10	20
Cultivating	5	10	15	10	20
Double digging	5	10	15		30
Preparing hole	5	10			30
Tilling	5	10			30
Turning compost	10	15	30	20	20
Pullups	5	5	8	8	
Dips		5	8	8	
Sit-ups		5	8	8	
Step-up box		5	8		
Arm lifts-milk jugs		5	8		
Other exercise		5	10		
Mowing lawn				60	
Harvesting	5	10	15	10	
Picking flowers		10	10	10	
Walking and enjoying		5	10	6	
	-----	-----	-----	-----	-----
Total minutes:	60	150	180	180	210

The following four charts provide graphic illustration of the cyclical nature of the Dynamic Gardening Way Program. The values are estimates from my personal observations based on a hundred percent being the total for that activity.

For example, in April, gardening exercise can amount to eighty percent of your total exercise output. If you live in the north this peak may be in May or June. If you live in the deep south, your best gardening exercise months may be December and January. Also, the value eighty percent is just an estimate. If you enjoy spring sports then your value will be lower. Subsequently, your cross-training percentage will be higher.

The main point is integrating Dynamic Gardening into your fitness lifestyle. While some may want to spend ninety percent of their time gardening, for others it may only be twenty percent. Perhaps all you want is a small patio garden with fresh greens, herbs and a few "Pixie" tomatoes. Either way, you're benefitting from gardening. Estimates are based on a garden in zone 7.

1. **Gardening Exercise chart.** Maximum output is in early spring with a gradual slowdown toward August and a small peak during late season clean-up activities. Amounts are percentage of total exercise.

2. **Circuit Training chart.** Use Circuit Training to balance muscle groups and increase strength. Circuit Training peaks should track slightly before or after gardening exercise peaks.

1. Amount of Exercise Chart

2. Circuit Training Chart

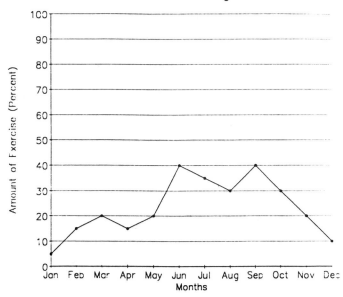

3. **Cross-Training chart.** Your particular cross-training activity will go here. Late fall and winter are the best times to expand the role of cross-training activities. Add volleyball, swimming, cross- country skiing or ice-skating to fill in the months between peak gardening and Circuit Training exercises. Gardening, Circuit Training and cross-training exercises will balance each other to provide a comprehensive aerobic and muscle-toning exercise program.

4. **Fresh Fruits and Vegetables Availability chart.** The three peaks illustrate a three-season garden with harvest peaks in May, July and October. Example is zone 7. Increase your gardening season with season extenders or a greenhouse. Freezing, canning and drying produce also will increase availability of garden fruits and vegetables, especially in the fall and winter months.

3. Cross-Training Chart

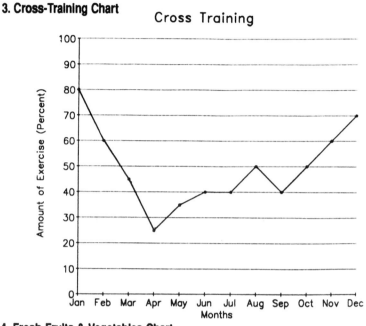

4. Fresh Fruits & Vegetables Chart

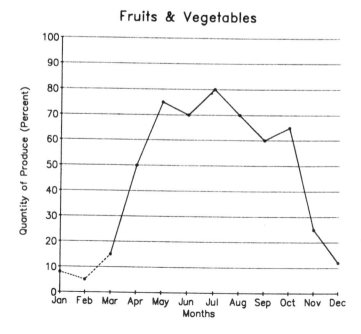

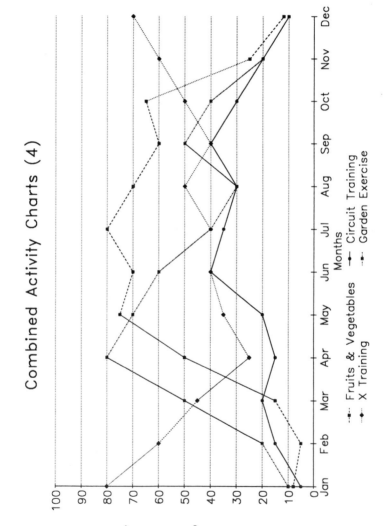

Combined Activity Charts (4)

Grape arbor/ Pullup bar Diagram

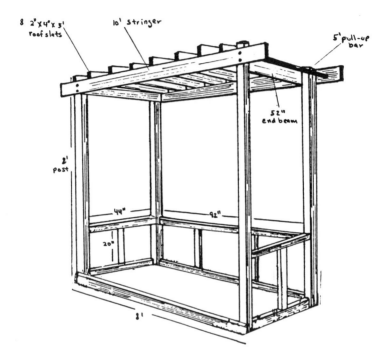

Note: I built this arbor in two weekends about two years ago. It was not assembled from a plan but built "free-form" (kind of like my garden). It has served me well, but I'm a much better gardener than architect. You can find plans for grape arbors in most gardening magazines. Just don't forget to add the pullup bar.

Grape Arbor/Pullup Bar

Parts List:

		QTY	SIZE
A	Posts	4	4" x 4" x 10'
B	Stringers	2	2" x 6" x 10'
C	End beams	2	2" x 6" x 52"
D	Roof slats	8	2" x 4" x 5'
E	Sitting rail—horizontal	1	2" x 4" x 92"
F	Sitting rail—horizontal	2	2" x 4" x 44"
G	Rail—posts	10	2" x 4" x 2'
H	Ground rail	2	2" x 6" x 8'
I	Ground rail	2	2" x 6" x 4'

Hardware:

	QTY	
Large carriage bolts	12	¼-20 x 6
Large washers	12	
Large nuts	12	
Plumbing pipe	1	¾" x 5'
Enamel spray paint	1	can

Dig post holes about 24 inches deep and 8' x 4' apart measured from the *center of the post*. Set posts into holes, and level plumb. Secure with lathe. Bolt 10' stringers to the posts on each side. Bolt in both 52" end beams. Nail a 2" x 6" ground rail to bottom of arbor on the outside.

The sitting rail sets inside the posts. The supporting posts are 24". They are nailed to the ground rail from the inside. Note that, although not illustrated, 2' x 2" x 4" support posts should be at each end of the three sitting rails nailed to the posts (6 supports plus the 4 illustrated). Nail roof slats into top beams.

Cut ¾" holes in one side of beams for pullup bar. Use file if holes are snug. Spray paint bar with rust-resistant paint. Insert bar into holes.

Dip Bar Diagram

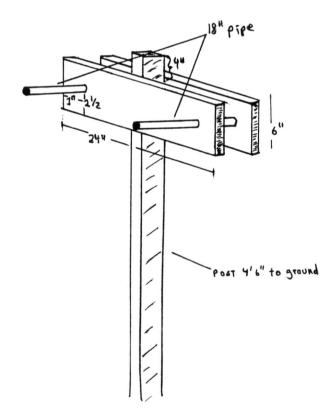

Dip bar

Parts List:

	QTY	SIZE
A Post	1	4" x 4" x 6'
B Wood sides	2	2" x 6" x 24"
Large screws (or bolts)	2	4"
Plumbing pipe	2	¾" x 18"
Enamel spray paint	1	can

Dig an eighteen inch hole for the 6' post and level. Secure to ground with cement. Drill ¾" holes for the pipe in both boards about 22" apart (width). The height of the post should be built to suit your height and arm length. An approximate height is 4' 6" if you're under six feet tall. If you're over six feet tall, you might want to use an 8' post, cut it to 7', set it twenty-four inches in the ground, and 5' above ground. Attach the wood sides to the post about four inches from the top with screws or bolts. Use nails to prevent movement.

When you're on the dip bar with arms extended, your feet should be one to two feet off the ground. If you have long arms you may want to set the bars wider than twenty-two inches. Paint pipes with a rust-resistant paint and insert into holes.

Sit-up board

Parts List:

	QTY	SIZE
A Exterior Plywood	1	¾" x 24" x 6'
B Braces	2	2" x 4" x 6'
C Braces	2	2" x 4" x 22"

Screws or Nails

Cut plywood to suit your height (average would be six feet), and sand edges smooth. Paint with water-resistant paint or staple a foam or plastic covering onto the surface. Nail or screw 2" x 4" braces underneath. Set the board up on bricks, boards or concrete blocks. Attach an elastic band or wood "T bar" to the far end to insert your feet under.

Sit-Up Board Diagram

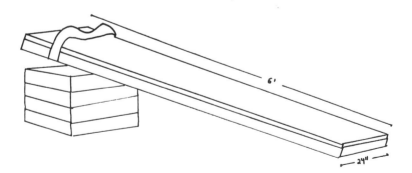

Chapter Eight

Analysis by Muscle Groups

I've organized the following tables by the muscle groups used during the gardening or circuit-training activity:

❀ arms
❀ chest
❀ back
❀ shoulders
❀ stomach
❀ legs

Gardening and circuit-training exercises can provide the same level of muscular development as traditional exercise programs using free weights or weight machines.

Bodybuilders pay careful attention to the muscle groups they exercise during each workout. Workouts are typically every other day—Monday, Wednesday and Friday; or Tuesday, Thursday and Saturday. They exercise each set of muscle groups during their one to two hour workout and rest them the next. On off days, they stretch, exercise aerobically or just relax. Muscles are "broken down" during a strenuous workout. The day off allows them to mend and grow.

You can work out *every day* by *alternating* muscle groups. For example, on Day One, exercise arms, back and shoulders. On Day Two, exercise legs and chest. Analyzing the muscle groups used during gardening and circuit training exercises allows you to transfer weight-training principles to Dynamic Gardening. The beauty of working out in the garden is that between sets you can harvest vegetables, weed, collect seeds, play with your children or pick flowers.

For example:

Alternating Day Exercises

Day One	Muscles used
Turn the compost pile	quadriceps, trapezius, deltoid, external oblique
Weed sitting down	flexor carpi radialis (forearm), deltoids

Day Two	Muscles Used
Chinups	latissimus dorsi, biceps
Sit ups	abdominal

Choose those exercises you enjoy the most, selecting at least two or three exercises from each muscle group. Feel free, of course, to make up your own. You're limited only by your imagination.

Muscles of the Body—Front View

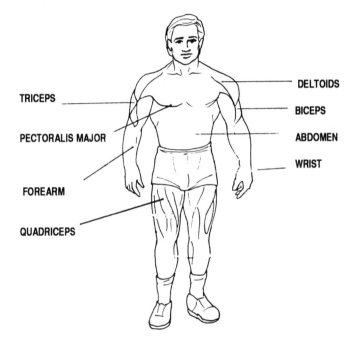

TRICEPS

PECTORALIS MAJOR

FOREARM

QUADRICEPS

DELTOIDS

BICEPS

ABDOMEN

WRIST

Muscles of the Body—Back View

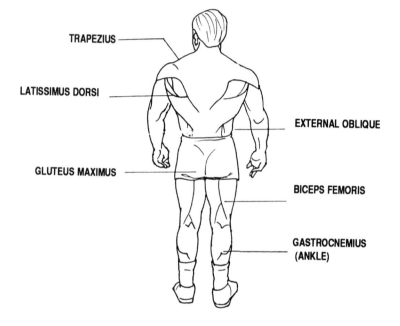

TRAPEZIUS

LATISSIMUS DORSI

EXTERNAL OBLIQUE

GLUTEUS MAXIMUS

BICEPS FEMORIS

GASTROCNEMIUS
(ANKLE)

Arms and Shoulders (1)

Gardening Exercise	Wrist	Forearms	Biceps	Triceps	Deltoids
hand weeding (sitting)	YES	YES	YES		YES
lunging & weeding	YES	YES	YES		YES
weeding using "The Stance"	YES	YES			YES
digging holes	YES	YES	YES		YES
turning compost	YES	YES	YES		YES
mowing lawn				YES	YES
chopping wood	YES	YES		YES	YES
pruning	YES	YES			YES
pushups				YES	YES

Arms and Shoulders (2)

Gardening Exercise	wrist	forearms	biceps	triceps	deltoids
raking, hoeing	YES	YES	(PULL IN)	(PUSH OUT)	YES
dips				YES	YES
using posthole digger		YES		YES	YES
chinups		YES	YES		YES
pullups		YES			YES
pulling mini-tiller backwards		YES	YES	YES	YES
raising & pushing wheelbarrow		YES	YES		YES
raising milk jugs to side		YES		YES	YES
climbing rope	YES	YES	YES		YES

Chest, Shoulders and Back

Gardening Exercise	Trapezius	Pectoralis major	Latissimus dorsi	Gluteus maximus
lunging & weeding				YES
weeding using "The Stance"			YES	YES
digging holes	YES			YES
turning compost	YES		YES	YES
chopping wood	YES	YES	YES	
push ups	YES	YES	YES	
raking, hoeing	YES		YES	
dips	YES	YES	YES	
posthole digging	YES	YES		
chinups	YES	YES	YES	
pullups	YES	YES	YES	
pulling mini-tiller backwards	YES	YES	YES	
raising/pushing cart	YES		YES	YES
climbing rope			YES	YES

Stomach and Legs

Gardening exercise	External oblique	Abdomen	Quadriceps	Ankle
lunging & weeding			YES	YES
weeding using "The Stance"	YES		YES	YES
digging holes			YES	YES
turning compost	YES	YES	YES	YES
mowing lawn			YES	YES
chopping wood		YES		
raking, hoeing			YES	YES
posthole digging			YES	YES
stepping up on box			YES	YES
situps	YES	YES		
leg raises (on dip bar)	YES	YES		
pulling mini-tiller backwards			YES	YES
raising & pushing wheelbarrow			YES	YES

Chapter Nine

Five-Year
Gardening and Exercise Plan

The following sample garden outlines a five-year plan that incorporates both gardening and Circuit-Training exercises. The reward for your effort will be a major portion of the fresh fruits and vegetables for a family of four each year. The five-year duration illustrates the long range nature of a health and wellness *lifestyle* versus a particular diet and exercise *program*. Use this as a guide to develop a plan that suits your individual needs.

The sample garden is organized by:

Exercise

Garden preparation and maintenance is listed under *exercise*. The first few years lean toward establishing and preparing new gardens: double digging beds, digging holes, cultivating soil, and turning compost. Once all garden beds are completed, the transition is toward maintenance activities.

Circuit Training

If you plan to add Circuit Training structures, set up a rope, step-up box, or sit-up board early in the season. As you progress, build the grape arbor and dip-bar structures. Once the garden is established, Circuit Training and cross-training play greater roles in maintaining fitness.

Planting

Each year select your favorite vegetables, flowers, berry bushes, fruit trees and herbs to plant. Using the organizational techniques in Chapter 22, plan your perennial beds; once established, they will produce for many years with relatively little effort. Each year keep busy with annual vegetables and flowers and transplanting existing perennial plants.

Harvest

For a quick harvest, choose vegetables that are easy to grow and productive: tomatoes, peppers, green beans, carrots, spinach and lettuce the first few seasons. Perennials require a year or more until first harvest. Beds planted today will yield fruits and vegetables one, two or three years later.

Years to Harvest

Berry bushes (1 to 2 years)	Perennial vegetables	Fruit trees (3 years)	Perennial herbs (1 year)	Grapes (1 to 2 years)
blueberries raspberries blackberries	asparagus (3 years) garlic (1 year) rhubarb (2 years)	apple peach cherry plum pear	sage rosemary thyme oregano	muscadine seedless

YEAR 1

Exercise

Dig and prepare two 4' x 8' or 3' x 12' deep-dug raised beds.
Construct compost bin.
Add compost, leaves, grass clippings, and food wastes.
Turn compost.
Weed, cultivate, and mulch garden.
Build sifter, cold frame, or potting bench.

Circuit-Training

Do sit-ups, pushups and step-up on box.
Construct grape arbor/pullup bar.
Do pullups and chinups.

Plant

Vegetables: lettuce, spinach, carrots, onions, tomatoes,
              bush beans, peppers.

Herbs: (A)   basil, summer savory and dill.
       (B)   parsley.
       (P)   oregano, sage, chives, garlic, thyme and rosemary.

Berry
bushes: blueberries.
Fruit trees: apple and pear.

Harvest

Vegetables: lettuce, spinach, carrots, onions, tomatoes, bush
              beans, peppers.

Herbs: All herbs above.

(A) Annual   (B) Biennial   (P) Perennial

YEAR 2

Exercise

Add two to four more deep-dug raised beds.
(Total four to six beds.)
Add one 10' x 10' square plot for corn and melons.
Add a strawberry bed.
Turn compost.
Construct dip bar.
Construct vertical structures for pole beans.

Circuit-Training

Do sit-ups, dips, pushups, chinups, pullups and step-up on box.

Plant

Vegetables: corn, melons and pole beans.
Flowers: small perennial flower bed.
Berry
 bushes   blackberry or raspberry bushes.
Fruit trees: peach, plum, cherry, nectarine and fig.
Grapes: grape vines around arbor.

Three Season Garden (add to garden above)

Spring: greens, cabbage and broccoli.
Summer: corn, pole beans and melons.
Fall: cabbage, broccoli, spinach, lettuce,
              collards, mustard greens, turnip greens and kale.

Harvest

All above with more herbs and a few blueberries.

YEAR 3

Exercise

Add two to four deep-dug raised beds (total six to ten beds).
Add one or two perennial flower beds.
Turn compost.

Circuit-Training

Do sit-ups, pushups, pullups, chinups, dips, leg raises (on dip bar) and step-up on box.

Add weight while doing pullups and dips.

Plant

Three season garden from year 2.

Add more difficult
vegetables: cauliflower, Brussels sprouts, and eggplant.

Add long-growing
vegetables: leeks, parsnips.

Establish perennial
beds: aquilegia, echinacea purpurea, rudbeckia, coreopsis, daisies, dianthus, achillea and other perennials that do well in your climate.

Harvest

Three season vegetables above.

Blueberries, blackberries or raspberries, apples, pears and grapes.

YEAR 4

Exercise

Add two deep-dug raised beds (Total 8-12).
Purchase chipper/shredder for composting leaves and tree limbs.
Turn compost.

Circuit-Training

Follow Year 3 Circuit-Training program.

Plant

Establish massed plantings of flowers. Start plants from seed.
Grow more difficult plants.

Replace any trees or bushes that have died.

Harvest

All vegetables and fruits above with addition of: strawberries, apples, pears, asparagus, blueberries, blackberries, raspberries, cherries, plums, and grapes.

YEAR 5

Exercise

Double dig or spot dig existing beds.
Exercise and garden as early as possible using season extenders, cold frames and hot beds.
Cultivate and maintain garden.

Turn compost.

Circuit-Training

Continue Circuit Training Program.
Add weights while doing pullups and dips.

Plant

Annual vegetables, flowers and herbs.

Transplant and divide existing perennial flowers. Trade or give extras to friends and neighbors.

Experiment with unusual or more difficult vegetables, fruits and herbs.

Harvest

Three-season vegetables above.
All fruits and berries above.

Chapter Ten

Sustainable and Intensive Gardening Techniques

This chapter introduces the techniques of sustainable and intensive gardening. Sustainable gardening emphasizes the soil and the use of natural fertilizers and pesticides. The term *sustainable agriculture* is often used synonymously with *organic* farming and gardening techniques. There are important differences.

Currently, the term "organic" means many things to many people. Most "certified organic" produce is grown on land that has not had chemical pesticides or synthetic fertilizers used for three to five years. Each state has its own particular requirements. A uniform legal definition of "organic" is currently being formulated by the Organic Farmers Association Council. Most organic gardeners use fertilizers and pesticides from natural sources while emphasizing the creation of a rich, porous soil. In this book I'll use the terms dynamic, sustainable, Integrated Pest Management (IPM), and the more familiar "organic" label to describe my gardening methods.

There is also a *Bio-Dynamic Method* of farming and gardening. First described by Rudolf Stein in Germany over fifty years ago, bio-dynamic practitioners view the entire farm as a single organism and adhere to strict rules for composting, and plant seeds by the phase and constellation of the moon. It is an interesting subset of organic gardening but has *no relationship* to the Dynamic Gardening Way.

The Techniques of Sustainable (organic) Gardening

Sustainable gardening and farming refers to "a system of agriculture that is ecologically, economically and socially viable, in the short as well as long-term. Rather than standing for a specific set of farming (gardening) practices, a sustainable agriculture represents the end-goal of developing a food production system that:

❀ Yields plentiful, affordable, high-quality food and other agricultural products.
❀ Does not deplete or damage natural resources (such as soil, water, wildlife, fossil fuels, or the germ plasm base).
❀ Promotes a healthy environment.
❀ Depends on energy from the sun and on natural biological processes for fertility and pest management.
❀ Can last indefinitely.[1]

Throughout this book, keep the word "sustainable" in your mind. Just as farming can be sustainable, so can your fitness program. To me, the analogy is clear—I've transferred my long-term approach to growing fruits and vegetables to my personal fitness lifestyle.

---

1. Source: Appropriate Technology Transfer for Rural Areas (ATTRA), "Sustainable Agriculture Concepts and Farm Applications: Attra Summary"

Intensive Gardening derives from the decades-old French-Intensive method where limited space yields maximum output. Intensive techniques feature raised beds, compost, vertical structures and an ultra-fertile soil. Plants are not grown in rows but intermixed with one another according to nutrient requirements and growth habits.

The most important point to remember is that there are many "organic gardening" techniques. And they vary widely. My goal is to provide you with enough information so you can use the technique that best suits your *fitness lifestyle*. The two most important gardening techniques are composting and creating raised, deep-dug beds. They are the foundation and lifeblood of a sustainable garden.

The Dynamic Gardening Way

Grow fresh fruits and vegetables with every ounce of your energy, yet without concern or worry about the size of your harvest.

Invite others to share in your joy of gardening, fully understanding that it's natural and expected that intelligent, good people can disagree.

Set long-term goals, yet focus entirely on the garden activity at hand.

Just looks like garbage to me . . .

Chapter Eleven

Composting and Raised Bed Gardening

Composting is the creation of humus from a collection of organic waste products. Creating compost requires the proper combination of: ingredients, material size, bin size, air, water, "turning" and macro and microorganisms.

Ingredients

The proper mix of nitrogen and carbon material is essential for proper decomposition and the "heating up" of the compost. The ratio of carbon to nitrogen should be 30 to 1. For each part of nitrogen, there should be thirty parts of carbon. This is not as difficult as it may sound. Simply mix "brown" carbon-based waste materials—leaves, sawdust, or straw, with "green" high-nitrogen waste materials—grass clippings, weeds, or manures. It's best to alternate materials in layers—large sticks on the bottom, grass clippings, leaves, soil, weeds, hay, and more soil. Continue layering until the pile is four to five feet high.

Size of Materials

Shred materials by mowing over them with a lawn mower, chopping them with a machete or using a commercial chipper/shredder. Smaller particles provide more surface area for microbial activity and decompose faster.

Water

The compost pile should always be damp. However, it should never be soggy or sit in water. Set large sticks or an old pallet in the bottom to ensure proper drainage. If the weather is dry, water every few days. During periods of prolonged rain, cover the compost bin with a plastic tarp.

Mass

Each bin should be at least three feet tall, wide and long. I typically pile compost over five feet high because light materials such as leaves or grass clippings are mostly air and decompose to a fraction of their original height in a few weeks. Enclosures can be built from treated wood and chicken wire. Materials and shapes for compost bins vary widely. Arrange chicken wire in a circle. Tie together used pallets, usually available for little or no cost. Set concrete blocks in a "U" shape. Commercial compost bins are also available locally or through mail order companies. Commercial compost bins are attractive, lightweight, and convenient.

Air

Aerobic decomposition will not occur without air penetrating throughout the compost pile. Place small branches, dead bushes and sunflower stalks on the bottom of the pile and in the center. This allows air to reach the center of the pile and prevents compaction of materials. Some gardeners insert sticks and sunflower stalks in the pile at different angles. Others use metal or plastic pipes with holes cut in the sides for ventilation.

Grass clippings can be mixed with leaves and soil and composted in plastic bags. However, unless there is sufficient drainage and aeration, decomposition will be anaerobic, and may produce an odor. *Anaerobic decomposition* occurs in the *absence of air* and produces methane gas. This is common with landfills, due mostly to their large mass, which prevents air from reaching the decomposing materials.

Turning the Compost Pile

"Turning" means moving the materials from one bin or container to another so the materials on the top and sides are moved to the center where they will heat up and decompose. It is best to have two or three separate bins. The first bin is for fresh waste products which are moved to the second bin and then turned a third time to the last bin. At that point you should have brown, crumbly compost. I use old newspaper pallets and tie ten together to form a three compartment compost bin. Sides are easy to remove and after a few years I replace all the pallets with new ones (and they're free!).

Turn the compost pile regularly. You can turn it daily, weekly, monthly or just a few times a year. One rule of thumb is when the compost pile cools off, turn it. Some avid organic gardeners turn the compost every day which, under ideal conditions, can create fresh compost in three weeks or less. A more reasonable goal is turning a portion of the pile each week during peak gardening exercise months. If you're busy in the summer with other activities, turn the compost pile in the spring and fall. Turn compost at least twice before adding to the garden.

The amount of grass clippings, leaves, and table scraps available will determine how much compost you can produce. Most neighbors will be happy to give you their excess leaves and grass clippings. If stables are nearby, compost manure with straw, leaves and sawdust.

If you provide the proper conditions above yet the pile fails to heat up, the problem is most likely not enough nitrogen. Add a high nitrogen source such as blood meal, cottonseed meal or kelp meal. If the amount of nitrogen is too high, your nose will tell you as excess ammonia is released into the air.

Macro and Microorganisms

Earthworms, insects, fungi, bacteria and microbes all break down the raw materials in the compost pile. These organisms are readily found in good topsoil and compost. If you're unsure of the quality of your soil, you may want to add a commercial bacterial compost starter to the compost.

Words of Caution

Never add the following to the compost pile:

- ❀ animal bones.
- ❀ grease or fat.
- ❀ meat scraps.
- ❀ cat and dog wastes (they could transmit viruses).
- ❀ barbecue briquette ashes (too much sulfur).
- ❀ grass clippings with recently applied herbicides.
- ❀ plants or weeds infected with a virus.

If herbicides have recently been used on your lawn, wait at least a month before using grass clippings in the compost pile. Compost the materials thoroughly (the pile will heat up several times) before adding to the garden.

Summary

Composting creates sweet-smelling, porous, nutrient-rich humus. Whatever method of gardening you choose, don't omit the compost pile. It's the foundation of a sustainable garden. In addition, turning the compost pile burns calories, builds strength, muscle mass, and transforms leaves and grass clippings into a valuable resource.

Composting reduces the vast amounts of organic materials dumped in our landfills each year. These valuable resources would be contaminated and lost forever as a soil conditioner and fertilizer. Mulching and composting returns valuable nutrients to the growing cycle where they nourish the plants and trees that produce fresh fruits and vegetables for our table.

If you wish to learn more about composting, I recommend *Backyard Composting* by Harmonious Technologies, Harmonious Press, 1992. $6.95 (800) 833-0720 EXT 47. This easy-to-read, ninety-seven page book contains up-to-date information on how to create compost for your garden.

Raised Beds

Instead of traditional rows, grow plants in raised, deeply-dug, highly-enriched beds. The preparation of these garden beds is essential to creating an optimal soil environment and an important component of the Dynamic Gardening Way exercise program.

The beds, three to four feet wide, are raised six to twelve inches. You can reach plants growing in the middle of the bed from either side without walking on the soil. Dig each bed two feet deep and back fill with topsoil and compost. Raise the bed with wood, plastic or brick frames. If materials are not available or cost is a factor, simply raise and contour the soil.

Don't feel limited by a square or rectangular design. Raised beds can assume any shape and be placed anywhere in the garden. Experiment with triangular, circular or free-form designs. Mix edible plants with ornamental flowers to create an interesting highlight in the garden.

Double digging

This is the below-the-ground preparation of raised garden beds. Prepare deep-dug beds by marking off a rectangular area of soil about four by six feet. Starting at the narrow end dig out a row of sod.

Figure 11.1 Cut out sod. Move to a wheelbarrow.

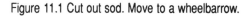

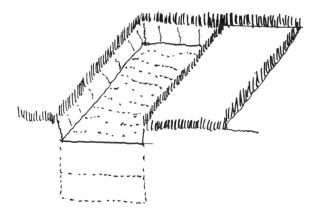

Dig out the soil, one spade length deep. Move this soil into a wheelbarrow.

Figure 11.2 Dig out first twelve inches of soil.

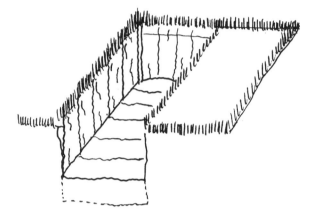

Increase the size and depth of the first trench so you can step down into it to dig another spade length deep. Dig the soil to a total depth of about two feet. This is the "double dig."

Figure 11.3 Dig out the second twelve inches of soil.

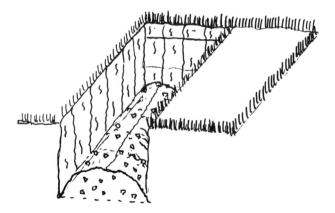

Cut out the sod from the second row and move it, upside down, to the bottom of the first.

Figure 11.4 Move sod from second row to first trench.

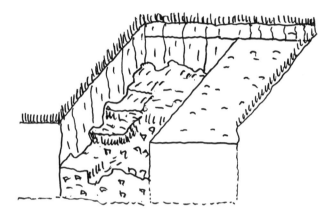

Dig out the first twelve inches of soil from the second trench and move to the first, mixing in compost, organic fertilizers, and coarse sand (if your soil needs added drainage).

Figure 11.5 Move soil from second trench to first.

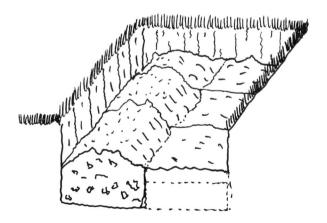

Dig out the second twelve inches of the second trench and move to the top of trench one. Raise the bed with good topsoil and compost. Continue digging to the right, cutting out sod and digging trenches. Add the sod and soil in the wheelbarrow to the last trench.

Figure 11.6 Finish second trench.

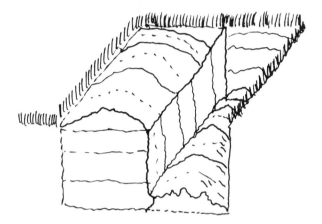

If you have sandy loam it will be relatively easy. If you have either clay or rocky soil, you may have to use a pick to break up the soil. This will take extra time. Set your goals accordingly. You might want to double dig one 4' x 8' or 3' x 12' bed in the spring and another in the fall. Double digging is vigorous exercise. Don't add unnecessary pressure by trying to dig to a certain depth, at a certain speed or more beds than you can handle. Be sure to use proper stance and grip while double digging. Take your time, pace yourself and quit when you're tired.

If you feel that double digging is not for you, then hire a landscaping service to double dig the initial garden beds. There are plenty of other gardening exercises you can enjoy.

Observe the difference between traditional row gardening and deep-dug, raised beds. Plants will be larger, produce longer, and withstand drought better.

Raised Beds versus Traditional Rows

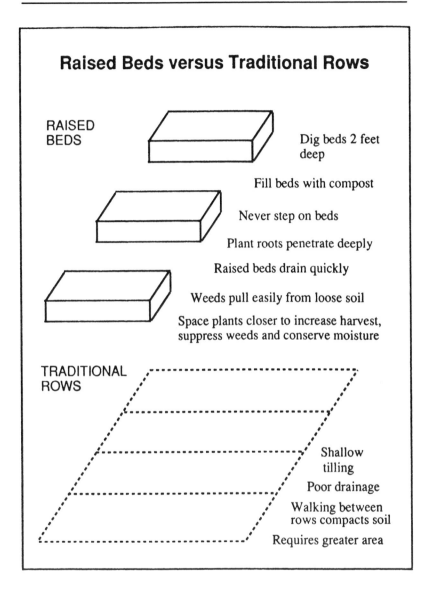

RAISED
BEDS

Dig beds 2 feet deep

Fill beds with compost

Never step on beds

Plant roots penetrate deeply

Raised beds drain quickly

Weeds pull easily from loose soil

Space plants closer to increase harvest, suppress weeds and conserve moisture

TRADITIONAL
ROWS

Shallow tilling

Poor drainage

Walking between rows compacts soil

Requires greater area

You can reduce *soil compaction* by never walking on double dug, raised beds. Foot traffic, rain, and heavy machinery all compact the soil, reducing the amount of water and air available to the roots. Loose, friable soil allows roots to travel deep into the ground.

Raised, deep-dug garden beds allow *closer spacing*, as much as three times closer than in a traditional garden. Closer spacing increases total yield, shades and cools the ground, and reduces weed growth between plants.

After only one season, the benefits of compost and double digging will be apparent. I am always amazed how many of my neighbors complain of poor tomato harvests during the drought and heat of summer. Meanwhile, my six-foot-tall tomato plants produce abundantly, obtaining nutrients and moisture from a root system that has penetrated the soil two to four feet deep.

Vertical structures are another means of maximizing space in a small garden. Wood or plastic-coated metal tomato stakes are good for tall-growing varieties. Commercial structures include nylon netting stretched across metal or wood posts. Build more durable vertical structures from PVC pipe or three-quarter-inch plumbing pipe. Tall vertical structures are good for pole beans, tomatoes, and peas.

Although not particularly attractive, discarded concrete reinforcing wire is very useful for a variety of vertical structures. It's available in six-foot lengths. Cut a large roll into six-foot-tall tomato cages with a diameter of 18" to 24". Grow beans and peas on them by bending the wire into a vertical "U" shape. Use four-foot sections for cucumbers, squash and cantaloupes.

Weeding Tools

Four of my favorite hand tools are the *long-handled scuffle hoe*, *Cape Cod weeder*, a *hand mattock* and a *hand weeder*. Always keep these tools sharp to optimize their cutting efficiency.

The scuffle hoe has a hinged, stirrup blade on a long handle. The blade is parallel to the ground and slices weeds at the soil line.

Figure 11.7 Scuffle hoe

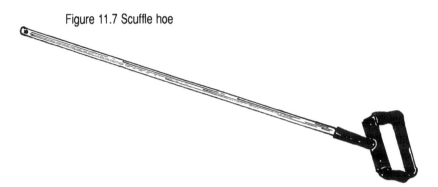

The Cape Cod weeder is an L-shaped tool on a short handle useful for digging out weeds and loosening soil between plants. This weeder is sturdy and has a thick blade. (Available from Gardener's Supply Company.)

Figure 11.8 Cape Cod weeder

The hand mattock is a heavy garden tool for digging out large weeds and spent vegetables. It is excellent for the "power" lunge and weed exercises, discussed in Chapter 6. (Available from most garden supply companies.)

Figure 11.9 Hand mattock

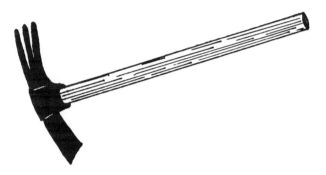

The hand weeder has a very thin, sharp blade ideal for slicing weeds at the soil line. (Available from Smith and Hawken.)

Figure 11.10 Hand weeder

Tilling

There are generally three different categories of tillers: front-tine, rear-tine and mini-tillers. Medium and large size front-and rear-tine tillers are best for traditional row gardens.

Rear-tine tillers are easier to maneuver than front-tine tillers due to the fact that they are pulled forward by their wheels. Typically weighing over one hundred pounds, they are best for gardens planted in straight rows. They're ideal for preparing medium to large gardens and turning under weeds.

Front-tine tillers require more muscle to maneuver and are not as steady as rear-tine tillers. The tines in front pull you forward as you walk behind the tiller. Front-tine tillers are typically less expensive than rear-tine tillers of the same horsepower.

Large tillers break up the soil to a depth of only six to ten inches. Tilling the same area twice will dig deeper. Use large tillers to prepare large plots for corn, melons, and other wide--space vegetables. They also are efficient for turning in "green manures"—cover crops grown for their soil-enriching properties. If you have the space, alternating green manures and productive vegetable beds each year is an excellent strategy for creating a nutrient-rich, porous soil.

Mini-tillers

These lightweight, labor-saving devices are useful for areas too small for the larger, traditional tillers. They are light enough for women and senior citizens to pick up and maneuver in narrow, raised beds. In addition, mini-tillers are typically not pushed forward like traditional tillers but are operated in a back and forth motion as you move backward. This motion exercises the upper back and chest muscles.

Mini-tillers have many uses:

❀ Creating a six to eight inch edge around flower beds, bushes and trees.

❀ Weeding between plant rows.

❀ Pulverizing hard clay soil.

❀ Mixing and turning the compost pile.

To use one in the compost pile, first shred the materials with a lawn mower or chipper/shredder. After the pile heats up once, use the tiller to pull the material from one bin to another. In a two-section compost bin, stand in the empty bin with the section separating them open, and set the mini-tiller on top of the pile. Pull the compost toward you with the tiller.

The Mantis™ tiller has serpentine tines that break up soil better than the bolo tines of traditional tillers. Mantis Manufacturing offers attachments to their mini-tiller that allow it to double as an edger, de-thatcher, edge trimmer and lawn aerator.

Combining Vegetables (and Herbs)

Interplant vegetables with complementary root systems, growth and feeding habits. Grow tomatoes with carrots, peas with corn, and lettuce and spinach between broccoli and cauliflower plants.

Companion planting places vegetables near one another because of one plant's ability to repel the pests of another. It is complementary to interplanting. More of an art than science, most favorable companions found in gardening magazines have not been tested. Many suggestions are "tradition" passed down from generation to generation. The following table is presented as a general guideline. Experiment with the suggestions listed and don't be afraid to try your own. (For more information on vegetable, fruit and herb allies, companions and enemies, consult Tanya Denkla's *Gardening at a Glance*, Wooden Angel Publishing, 1991. 1-800-345-0096)

Quick List of Happy Companions and Unhappy Neighbors

Plant	Plant with:	Keep away from:
cabbage, broccoli, cauliflower	dill, chamomile, sage, rosemary, mint, and oregano.	pole beans, strawberry
tomatoes	asparagus, basil, mint, carrot	broccoli, corn
peppers and eggplant	tomatoes, beans, basil, onions and carrots.	brassicas, corn
squash	radishes, nasturtiums, corn	potato, pumpkin
potatoes	marigold, beans, corn and cabbage	pumpkins, tomatoes raspberries, spinach and cucumbers.
radishes	zucchini, cucumbers and melons.	
beets	bush beans, cabbage, lettuce and onions.	
soybeans	grow with anything	
onions, garlic, shallots, chives	summer savory, brassicas, carrots and spinach	peas, sage and beans
basil	tomatoes	rue
dill	cabbage	carrots, fennel
sage	All brassicas, carrots, tomatoes	cucumber, onion family
pyrethrum	grow with everything	
sunflower	cucumbers	potatoes and pole beans (all legumes)

Chapter Twelve

Sustainable Gardening
and
Integrated Pest Management

Sustainable gardening

A long-term gardening approach emphasizes feeding the soil instead of just feeding the plants with chemical fertilizers. Living soil organisms—earthworms, fungi, molds, actinomycetes and bacteria—break down organic matter slowly into nutrients that plants can easily assimilate. Nutrients may often be available in the soil, but because of improper pH or other factors, aren't available to the plants. Adding organic matter helps free up nutrients.

Feeding the soil sets in motion a process that is self replenishing. Earthworms both aerate and increase nutrients in the soil. Organic matter decomposes, providing nutrients slowly and naturally. Spent vegetables, weeds, and table scraps are composted and returned to the garden.

Fertilizers

Plants need three *macronutrients*: nitrogen (N), phosphorus (P) and potassium (K). Commonly referred to as NPK, the percentages of each are listed on fertilizer bags. For example, 13-13-13 contains thirteen percent by weight of nitrogen, phosphorus and potassium. Nitrogen is necessary for strong, green leaves and stems. Phosphorus is essential for fruit and flower production, strong roots and resistance to disease. Potassium, or potash (K_2O) helps plants manufacture sugar, ensuring strong roots and stalks that can withstand disease and drought.

141

There is much controversy about the advantages and disadvantages of synthetic versus natural fertilizers. Most chemical proponents argue that plants cannot distinguish between natural and chemical sources of these nutrients. I won't dispute that. But macro and micronutrients are seldom found alone. They are more often in solution in the soil or as part of a chemical compound. Improving soil tilth helps make these elements available to the plants.

Synthetic fertilizers provide a quick fix, a short-term dose of nutrients to the plants. In certain cases, this may be desirable or necessary. However, synthetic fertilizers must be replenished each year. Remember the term *sustainable?* Using chemical fertilizers in your garden is analogous to using pills, powders and prepackaged meals for your diet and fitness program. Both are not *sustainable.* They may provide short-term benefits but are a costly strategy over ten, twenty and fifty years.

In addition, if you *omit* composting, double digging, mulching and other techniques that foster an optimal soil environment, and simply substitute bagged organic fertilizers for 13-13-13, you lose many of the exercise benefits. At issue is not chemical versus natural but a long-term versus a short-term focus; soil enhancement versus plant nourishment; and lifestyle versus activity.

Organic Fertilizers
Organic fertilizers are now available through local garden centers as well as mail-order firms. Blood, bone, cottonseed and fish meal, bat guano, cricket manure, and earthworm castings are all good organic fertilizers. Horse, cow, and chicken manure are all good sources of nitrogen but should be composted before adding to the garden to both reduce weed seeds and avoid burning plants.

Calcium and iron can tie up phosphorus in the soil. Humic acids in organic matter convert insoluble phosphorus to a form plants can use.

A host of options for organic fertilizers abound. One source is the *local zoo.* A single elephant produces over 300,000 pounds of manure a year! *Breweries* produce spent hops. *Leather processing plants* produce leather tankage. Hair from a *barber shop* can be used as a slow-release, high-nitrogen fertilizer. A friend of mine gathered several hundred pounds of bat guano from a *cave*. The bats didn't even mind.

Mix *shredded newspaper* with a high nitrogen material such as blood meal or cottonseed meal. Avoid using any glossy multicolored fliers. They may contain harmful chemicals. Add plenty of soil to this mixture to create compost.

Start an *earthworm farm* in a shaded area. Sink a decay-resistant wood frame into the ground about five to six inches, filled with topsoil, newspapers, coffee grounds and shredded leaves. Keep the bed cool and moist. Feed the worms periodically with table scraps, coffee grounds and shredded leaves. Earthworms increase the fertility of the soil two to three times its original level.

Greensand or glauconite is an excellent source of potash. It contains over thirty micronutrients. It's a long-term solution—greensand takes years to release nutrients to the soil.

Finally, *mail-order firms* sell organic fertilizers in bulk. Nitron Industries, Maxicrop and Gardeners Supply Company sell organic fertilizers—including fish meal, sea kelp and greensand—at reasonable prices.

If you wish to learn more about organic fertilizers and pesticides, I recommend the excellent books on organic gardening and sustainable agriculture listed in the Appendix.

Home Garden is Not a Farm

Many beginning gardeners attempt to create a "miniature farm" in their back yards. The gardening methods and vegetable varieties available to a home gardener are often impractical for the commercial farmer. A sustainable garden is much different from a farm or even an organic farm. The chart on the next page sums up the differences.

Home Garden is *Not* a Farm

Farmer	Home gardener
Large quantities of one crop.	May grow small quantities of a wide variety of vegetables.
Pesticides may be necessary.	May be willing to accept some damage or lower yield to reduce pesticide use.
Can market only blemish-free produce.	Can grow vegetables for optimum nutrition and taste. Appearance is secondary.
Mono-culture both traditional and more convenient.	Interplanting of vegetables beneficial and desirable.
Large areas require heavy machinery.	Smaller areas favor raised, deep-dug garden beds, eliminating soil compaction.
Large areas favor symmetrical rows worked by machinery.	Small spaces allow irregular shapes, manual cultivating.
Subsistence depends on successful harvest.	Options of growing ornamental, experimental, and unusual varieties just for "fun."
Crops must be cost effective to grow.	Can grow long-season vegetables, such as leeks and parsnips.
Must use all space productively.	Can grow flowers and other plants purely for aesthetic value.

Integrated Pest Management (IPM)

Pesticides

One of the many misconceptions about organic methods is that pesticides are never used. Pests are free to devour our crops while we sit idly by worrying about the rain forests. This is not true. The IPM approach to pest control is multifaceted, comprehensive and balanced. Mechanical barriers, such as Reemay™, and sticky traps are safe and effective against certain insects. Interplanting and companion planting are used to confuse and ward off insect pests. Beneficial insects are encouraged to feed on harmful ones.

Chemical Pesticides

Eliminating chemical pesticides is the main target of many organic gardeners. Pesticides pose three separate yet related concerns, whether they are natural *or* chemical.

Persistence in the soil refers to how long the substance remains in the soil and food chain. The longer the toxin persists the greater the danger to the environment.

Toxicity is how lethal the pesticide is to non-target organisms. Toxicity categories include both skin and oral consumption values. Broad-spectrum insecticides kill beneficial insects as well as harmful ones. This upsets the equilibrium of the garden. In addition, the highly toxic pesticides, in relatively small doses, will kill fish, birds and mammals.

Residues on vegetables is the amount of chemical pesticides we eat. Some pesticides decay from exposure to sun and air. Cleaning and washing vegetables helps reduce levels of pesticide traces.

Each concern above presents a unique set of problems. If your major concern is *soil persistence,* then organic pesticides are definitely superior. They decay quickly, often in one day. The persistence of chemical pesticides varies greatly, therefore some chemical pesticides are worse than others. If you cannot eliminate chemical pesticides, at least choose those that decay quickly.

If your concern is *toxicity* then learn the LD_{50} values below. Note that a naturally-derived pesticide can be *more toxic* than its chemical counterpart. Also, in select cases, a chemical alternative may be preferred to organic pest control.

Imadan, a chemical pesticide, is suggested by some experts as an environmentally safer alternative to multiple sprayings with organic mixtures to protect fruit trees from the plum curculio. It is more effective and requires fewer sprayings than organic alternatives. Overall, it will have less impact on non-target populations.

Mechanical and organic controls should *always* be your first choice. Some organic pesticides, particularly *Bacillus thuringiensis* (Bt), are target specific and will not harm birds, fish or humans. However, if insect pests threaten to wipe out your entire apple crop, chemical pesticides may be warranted. Will you still reap the exercise benefits? Of course. Will the apples be healthy and nutritious to eat? Certainly. Using chemical pesticides or synthetic fertilizers would disqualify you as a "Certified Organic" farmer in those states that have an organic certification. Most organic gardeners would disapprove. However, that won't prevent you from realizing the health benefits of *Fitness the Dynamic Gardening Way*.

The last concern is chemical pesticide residues on your food. Below is a list of strategies to address this issue:

❀ Grow your own vegetables without chemical pesticides.
❀ Purchase vegetables from a local Certified Organic farmer. Some local farmers offer cooperative arrangements where they supply your family with vegetables during the year for a fixed price.
❀ Purchase Certified Organic fruits and vegetables from a local health food store.
❀ Wash fresh, store-bought vegetables thoroughly and purchase regionally grown, in-season vegetables. (Imported vegetables may be sprayed with pesticides long banned in the United States.)

Toxicity Category and LD_{50} Values.

The Environmental Protection Agency uses acute LD_{50} values to determine the toxicity category and the subsequent labeling of products. LD_{50} is the dosage that kills one-half of the test animals, typically rats or rabbits. LD_{50} is measured in milligrams of chemical tested per kilogram(mg/kg) of animal. One part per million (ppm) is equal to one mg/kg The LD_{50} value is usually determined for the technical substance rather than the formulated product. The *lower* the LD_{50}, the *more* toxic the substance.

The four categories of toxicity are:

CLASS 1   **Highly toxic**

"DANGER POISON"
Skull and crossbones on label.
Antidote statement.

CLASS 2   **Moderately toxic**

"WARNING"
No antidote statement.

CLASS 3   **Low-order toxicity**

"CAUTION"
(Slightly toxic)
No antidote statement.

CLASS 4   **Comparatively free from danger**

No warning, caution or antidote.

Selected Examples of Chemical Pesticides Ranked by Toxicity:

CLASS 1 Highly Toxic

NAME	LD$_{50}$	TRADE NAME	COMMENTS
Systox	2.5 - 6	Demeton™	Highly toxic.
Endosulfan	30-110	Thiogard 3™	Used to control aphids, Colorado potato beetles, flea beetles & leafhoppers.

CLASS 2 Moderately Toxic

NAME	LD$_{50}$	TRADE NAME	COMMENTS
Chlorpyrifos	96-270	Dursban™	Persists longer than 6 months.
Dimethoate	215	Cygon™, Rebelate™ & De-Fend™	An organophosphate insecticide, controls aphids and thrips.
Diazinon	300-400		An organophosphate, controls soil-inhabiting and other insects: onion maggots, thrips, aphids, and wireworms,
Dicofol	820-960	Kelthane™	Kills spider mites.

CLASS 3 Low Order Toxicity

NAME	LD$_{50}$	TRADE NAME	COMMENTS
Carbaryl * **	246-307	Sevin™	A carbamate insecticide, persists in the soil 1 to 6 months. Effective against aphids, Colorado potato beetles, flea beetles and leafhoppers.
Malathion **	1,375		An organophosphate, residues disappear quickly. Controls aphids, spider mites, bean beetles and stink bugs.
Methoxychlor	6000	Marlate™	Effective against most soft-bodied insects.

* Carbaryl/Sevin™ - Mites may develop a tolerance to it. It is highly toxic to bees.

** There is evidence that continued exposure to Malathion and Sevin™ may affect cholinesterase levels in the blood. Cholinesterase is a body enzyme necessary for proper nerve function. Malathion and carbaryl are less persistent in the soil than the pesticide they replaced (DDT) but are more water soluble.

Source: the University of Tennessee Agricultural Extension Service. PB595.

Dynamic Gardening Approach to Pest Management

Integrated Pest Management (IPM) techniques prescribe an orderly series of steps to reduce insect damage with minimal reduction of beneficial insect populations and the environment. Where IPM and organic gardening depart is that IPM practitioners will use chemical pesticides as a *last resort*. The focus is not natural versus chemical but a practical approach to obtaining a crop with minimal effect on the environment.

The organic approach to insecticides varies widely. Some organic gardeners advocate hand-picking insects from plants as their chief method of pest control. Others may use rotenone, a Class 2 organic pesticide, once or twice a week.

Strong, Healthy Plants

Healthy plants are the first line of defense against insect pests. While this may be stating the obvious, it reinforces the point that all the techniques of dynamic gardening, particularly composting and double digging, play a role in reducing damage from pests. Strong, healthy plants build natural defenses against insect predators. The weakest plants are the first to be infested.

Grow *disease-resistant* varieties. A plant ravaged by fusarium or verticillium wilt will be easy prey for insect pests. *Weeds* harbor insect pests and compete for nutrients. Eliminating weeds helps reduce harmful insect populations.

Mechanical Deterrents

Reemay™ and Agronet™ *floating row covers* protect plants from insect pests yet allow light, air and water to nourish crops. Row covers are made from a variety of substances: UV-stabilized polypropylene, spun-bonded polyester and extruded polyethylene. In the early spring, use row covers to keep spinach, Swiss chard and other green leafy vegetables blemish-free. Cover squash plants in early spring to prevent the squash vine borer from destroying the plants. Remove the row cover when the first flowers appear. *Sticky Traps* are simple but effective. They use colored paper or plastic strips with a sticky substance on the surface. Yellow attracts whiteflies and white attracts flea beetles.

Dormant Oil Spray

Spray during the fall, winter and early spring months to control insect pests on ornamental and fruit trees. Use in early spring before buds are open and when insects are just becoming active. Dormant oil controls aphids, whiteflies, mealybugs, scales, mites, thrips, and pear psyllids. It is not a poison, but kills insects by suffocating them. Insects cannot develop a tolerance to dormant oil.

Diatomaceous Earth

Not the type used in pool filters, it is the ground-up silicate skeletons of prehistoric one-celled organisms. It kills insect pests by piercing their bodies, causing them to dehydrate. It is most effective against soft-bodied insects such as aphids, slugs, mealybugs and whiteflies. Be sure to avoid inhaling any of the dust from diatomaceous earth.

Beneficial Insects

Trichogramma wasps are tiny parasites of insect pest eggs that are harmless to animals and humans. The larvae of *green lacewings* are effective in reducing aphids, mealybugs, whiteflies and the eggs of mites and thrips. Both the adult and larvae form of *ladybugs* prey on aphids.

The *praying mantis* preys on grasshoppers, caterpillars and other leaf-eating pests. This fascinating insect is fun to watch and has a unique, human-like quality as it moves its head and grasps its prey with its front legs. One year I bought and then stored mantis egg cases in the refrigerator before setting them out in mid-May. In mid-June I watched in amazement as hundreds of tiny mantises crawled out of their egg cases. During the summer, I spotted an adult mantis only several times in the garden. While cleaning the garden in the fall, I found four mantis egg cases on the tomato cages. The eggs proved that although difficult to find, the praying mantises were present in the garden.

Honey . . . maybe you're taking this organic business a little too far . . .

If the use of beneficial insects is part of your strategy to reduce insect pests, be sure to grow a variety of trees, bushes, and wildflowers to provide a safe haven from predators. Fennel, parsley, dill, borage, nasturtium, alyssum, hairy vetch and crimson clover all attract and harbor beneficial insects. Tall-growing native grasses, Echinacea (purple coneflower) and Rudbeckia (black-eyed Susan) are all attractive to bees, butterflies and other beneficial insects.

Non-toxic Deterrents

Safer™ Insecticidal Soap is based on fatty acids and effective against soft-bodied insect pests such as aphids yet harmless to mammals. Soaps break down surface tension on an insect's body and allow water and other irritants to penetrate it. I've used a mixture of soap, garlic, onion and pepper juice on my plants as a natural deterrent to insect pests.

Beneficial Nematodes and Bacterium

While some *nematodes* are harmful to plants, there are also beneficial strains, Hh and Nc. These nematodes attack the soil-dwelling grub of Japanese beetles, black vine weevils, cutworms, June beetles, and Oriental beetles. Beneficial nematodes are available from *Garden's Alive* listed in the Appendix.

Bacillus Thuringiensis (Bt) is a safe, naturally occurring bacterium effective against most caterpillars, such as the tomato hornworm and cabbage worms. Bt does not kill insects on contact, but once ingested, disrupts the circulatory system, causing death. Birds and beneficial insects are not affected, even after eating Bt-infected insects. Bt is harmless to humans, pets, and aquatic life, and leaves no harmful residues in the soil. It is sold under a number of trade names: Dipel, Thuricide, Bactospeine, and Bactur.

Bacillus Popilliae, also known as "milky spore disease," is a safe treatment for lawns and gardens. It effectively eradicates the grub of Japanese beetles, rose chafer, oriental beetles and some May and June beetles, yet is non-toxic to animals.

Organic Pesticides

Botanical insecticides are derived from the leaves, flowers, roots and seeds of plants. Whenever possible, substitute a botanical insecticide for a chemical one.

The three main benefits of natural pesticides is that they break down quickly in the soil from exposure to light and air; they will not add toxicity to the soil to be carried further into the food chain; and are generally less toxic to non-target populations.

The following chart lists organic pesticides by toxicity. Many are available in lawn and garden centers nationwide. If you cannot find them locally, a listing of mail order suppliers is provided in the Appendix.

CLASS 2 Moderately Toxic

NAME	LD$_{50}$	COMMENTS
Rotenone	60-132	Derived from the roots of tropical legumes such as derris and cube. Residues break down within five days from exposure to light and oxygen. A broad spectrum insecticide, rotenone is more toxic than the chemical pesticides Malathion or Carbaryl. It is toxic to fish and should not be used where it could contaminate streams or ponds. Rotenone is a contact and stomach poison effective on flies, thrips, fleas, imported cabbageworms, cabbage loopers, slugs, weevils and beetles. Rotenone should be used only as a last resort.

CLASS 2 Moderately Toxic

NAME	LD$_{50}$	COMMENTS
Phosmet (Imadan) (chemical exception)	147-316	Is a moderately toxic chemical pesticide but recommended by several sources as the safest, most effective method of eradicating plum curculio from apples, peaches, plums and other stone fruits. It has a relatively short residual effect and has little impact on beneficial insect populations.

CLASS 3 Low Order Toxicity

NAME	LD$_{50}$	COMMENTS
Sabadilla	400	Is derived from the seeds of the tropical plant, *Schoenocaulon officinale*. It is particularly effective against squash bugs, harlequin bugs, cucumber beetles and grasshoppers. Sabadilla is both a contact and stomach poison to insects.
Ryania	750	Is derived from the tropical shrub, *Ryania speciosa*. An alkaloid, insects stop feeding soon after ingestion and typically die within 24 hours. It controls aphids, corn borers, flea beatles, leafhoppers, and Mexican bean beetles and many fruit and foliage eating caterpillars.
Pyrethrum	200-1500	Is derived from the flower heads of the plant, *Chrysanthemum spp*. A contact insecticide, pyrethrum will down flying insects, however, if the dosage is not strong enough, the insects will revive. Therefore, it is often combined with a more lethal insecticide such as rotenone.

Summary

In the context of a healthy lifestyle, Integrated Pest Management (IPM) and sustainable gardening techniques offer many benefits. We can simultaneously care for the environment, the soil, the plants we grow *and* our bodies. Composting and double digging provide exercise, convert waste materials to a valuable resource and increase overall harvest. Organic fertilizers and soil conditioners improve the long-term quality of the soil reducing the need to add fertilizers each year. Substituting alternative pest management strategies rather than relying on broad-spectrum chemical pesticides has less impact on the environment and non-target populations.

The Dynamic Gardening Way

Exercise and eat proper foods with the intention of losing or maintaining an appropriate weight—yet never step on a scale.

Strive to improve yourself, but not because you feel you have to, you should, or you need to, but because you're celebrating your awareness, which makes you a worthwhile, important human being.

Fitness is not who's faster, stronger or bigger. It is the integration of mind, body and spirit, to promote a healthy, happy, long life.

Chapter Thirteen

Plant Propagation Techniques

Propagating plants offers considerable savings, additional variety, and additional activity during the fall, winter and early spring months. While starting plants from seed is the most common method, it's not the only one. Some plants self-sow, and others are started from bulbs, tubers, and rhizomes.

Starting Plants from Seed

I trace my transition from a frustrated amateur gardener to an accomplished one when I learned a consistent method of growing plants from seed. For years I attempted to start plants from seed in small plastic pots on a south-facing windowsill. Every year the plants grew tall and spindly. Many never germinated. The soil in the small plastic pots dried out, and the plants died if I missed watering them for a single day. When I transplanted the plants to the garden, most died or did not produce well. It's a wonder I didn't give up in disgust and take up golf!

The problem with starting plants on a windowsill is that it is too cold at night and too hot during the day. During the day, a plant on a southern-facing window heats up ten to fifteen degrees greater than the indoor room temperature. Still, the plant does not receive sufficient light, particularly on cloudy days. Weak, spindly plants result.

The Accelerated Propagation System (APS), available from Gardener's Supply Company, is the best method to start plants from seeds I've ever used. Yes, I'm sold. The APS is one of the best gardening and, yes, *fitness investments* you'll ever make. These self-contained kits include a tray that holds about two quarts of water. Plant cells, available in twenty-four and forty cell models, rest on a capillary matting that sits in the tray, providing the plants with moisture from the bottom without drowning their roots. The trays hold water for about two weeks. A clear plastic dome is set over the cells to create a mini-greenhouse environment.

Accelerated Propagation System (APS)

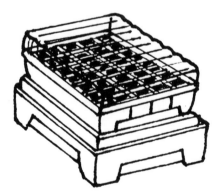

Use a greenhouse or fluorescent lights to provide light to the plants. If your outside temperature is consistent in early spring or fall you might want to experiment with placing the APS outside in a protected, shaded area. However, direct sunlight and temperatures above 80 degrees will bake the emerging seedlings under the clear plastic dome.

A fluorescent light, set to be on for fourteen to sixteen hours a day with an automatic timer, will provide adequate light and ensure a constant temperature. Specially designed, full-spectrum lights are available. I've never used these and have always had good results with inexpensive, shop-light bulbs.

The first two leaves of a plant are called cotyledon leaves. After the plants develop true leaves (usually the third and fourth leaves), pick up the trays every few days to prevent the roots from growing into the mats. When the seedlings are too large for their cells, transplant them to individual pots or their permanent garden beds. Sometimes I simply set the trays (without the plastic dome) outside to harden off. Keep the plants away from direct sunlight, preferably in filtered light or full shade. After about a week outside, transplant the seedlings to the garden.

For the past several years I've tested new plant varieties in the Southeast for *Organic Gardening* magazine. The APS has been an invaluable tool in starting seeds quickly and reliably. I have grown a wide variety of indoor and outdoor plants, herbs and bushes: cacti, cyclamen, African violets, marjoram, summer savory, thyme, sage, tomatoes, peppers, eggplant, and crepe myrtle.

With a setup of nine APS units I can start between 200 and 300 plants every six to eight weeks, all for the cost of potting soil and seed packets. In addition, I've collected seeds from my garden, my neighbors' gardens, and several botanical gardens and grown hundreds of perennials from seed—essentially free.

My Favorite Plants to Start From Seed.

Herbs		
Variety	**Type**	**Comments**
Basil	A	Very easy, good for pesto.
Borage	A	Very easy, large seeds, self-sows, attracts bees.
Dill	A	Easy, self-sows, used for pickling.
Lemon balm	P	Easy, spreads.
Oregano	P	Moderately easy, good for Italian cuisine. spreads.
Parsley	B	Fine seeds, slow to germinate, likes cool weather.
Sage	P	Easy, likes a partially shaded area in hot climates.
Winter savory	P	Easy, used in soups and stews.

(A) Annual   (B) Biennial   (P) Perennial

Seed Starting Mix

Several commercial seed starting mixtures are available. Starting mixes vary widely in composition. I've had good luck with Hyponex™ and Bacto™ Professional potting soil mixes. Feel the bag when you're unsure of the quality. The mix should be light, porous, and break apart easily. Ordinary soil from the garden is not recommended. It may contain a soilborne fungus that can cause *damping off* that kills seedlings. Typically it causes seedling to pinch at the base, fall over and die.

Perennial Flowers	
Fountain grass	Slow-growing, takes two years to mature.
Shasta daisy	Easy to grow, hardy.
Rudbeckia	"black eyed Susan", easy, colorful.
Coreopsis	Easy, spreads, tolerates neglect.
Echinacea purpurea	"purple coneflower" Easy, tall plants, collect seeds in fall.
Stokesia	Easy, slow-growing from seed.
Blackberry lilies	Easy, three to four weeks to germinate.
Aquilegia	Slow-growing, fragile, take two weeks to mature. Attractive flowers.
Physostegia	Easy, spreads, tolerates neglect.

If you wish to create your own soil-less mixture, four potting mix amendments are useful. *Vermiculite* is porous, light and retains moisture. Mined in Georgia, it has a nearly neutral pH (7.0—7.5) and doesn't tie up micronutrients. Use it to cover very fine seeds. I purchase the largest bag I can find and add it to commercial mixes when they feel too heavy. *Peat moss* is shredded, decayed wood harvested from swampy peat bogs. Peat is light, retains water, and is somewhat acidic. *Perlite* is a light, white, non-porous soil amendment used for aerating and keeping a soil mix light. Use in soil mixes for plants that do not like their roots standing in water: African violets, gloxinia, and cactus. *Sand* has large silicon granules; add to a soil mixture when you need weight and drainage.

Annual Vegetables	
Tomatoes	Very easy, grows quickly. Transplant to larger pots as soon as true leaves appear.
Peppers	Easy, grow six to eight weeks before last frost date.
Zucchini	Easy, germinates and grows quickly.
Cucumbers	Easy, germinates and grows quickly.
Broccoli	Easy, grows slowly; start six to eight weeks before last frost date in spring.
Cauliflower	Easy, same as broccoli, above.
Cabbage	Easy, same as broccoli, above.
Lettuce	Easy, some varieties need light to germinate; cover with light cover of vermiculite.
Spinach	Easy.
Melons	Easy, large seeds; germinates and grows quickly.

Create a soil-less mix with three parts peat moss, two parts vermiculite, one part perlite, and one part sand. Experiment with your own combinations or add amendments to existing commercial mixtures.

Seed Germination

Seeds fail to germinate for a number of reasons. Beets, Swiss chard, cacti, and some lily seeds require scarification to germinate. Scar seeds with a file or by rubbing between a folded piece of sandpaper.

Some perennial seeds require a period of cold before germinating. If your germination rate is poor try mixing seeds with vermiculite in a small cup, soaking and draining the seeds, and placing the cup in the refrigerator for two to three weeks. The period of cold simulates winter conditions and may increase the germination rate.

Other Propagation Methods:

Annuals that self-sow and return year after year.

Vegetables	Flowers	Herbs
Cucumbers	Zinnia	Borage
Tomatoes	Calendula	Chamomile
Zucchini	Statice	Dill
Lettuce	Foxgloves	Feverfew
Radishes	Forget-me-nots	
	Vinca	

Grow spreading plants in a wood enclosure, a plastic pot with the bottom cut out or in a window box by themselves. I have several patches of spearmint, lemon balm, tansy, phyostegia and Jerusalem artichokes that have spread considerably over the years. The mint has escaped from my garden and is now invading my neighbor's yard!

Plants that Propagate by Stolons, Runners, Rhizomes and Tubers.

Vegetables/Fruits	Flowers	Herbs
Asparagus: propagated by second or third year roots.	Physostegia virgiana	Mint family Lemon balm
Strawberries: propagated by runners.	Artemisia	Bee balm (*Monarda didyma*)
Jerusalem artichokes: spread by underground tubers.	Soapwort	Oregano
Black raspberries: propagate by rooting their stem tips back into the ground.		Lamb's ears (Stachys byzantina)
		Thyme
		Tansy

Moving Plants Outside

Hardening plants off refers to acclimating plants started from seeds indoors to sun, wind, drought, and insect pests. Instead of moving seedlings directly from indoor conditions to their permanent garden location, move to a protected staging area for a week or two. I've used cold frames, row covers and a shaded area next to a fence to harden off plants.

Use a *cold frame* to harden off and grow early spring vegetables and protect them from killing frosts. Cold frames can be constructed from a variety of materials:

 ❀ A wood box with a glass or plastic lid that can be opened from the top.
 ❀ Aluminum and plastic frame models with a UV protected plastic covering.
 ❀ Cinder blocks and an old glass sliding door for a lid.

A *hot bed* is a cold frame with a heat source. Paint fifty gallon drums or plastic milk jugs black, fill with water, and set them at the south side of your hot bed. The water will absorb heat from the sun and warm the plants. You can buy an electrical heat tape with a thermostat that opens when the soil temperature falls below freezing temperatures. A tape imbedded in the soil will warm and protect plants.

An enclosed compost pile can heat a hot bed. Construct a hoop "cloche" with half-inch, flexible PVC piping and clear plastic. Insert both ends of the PVC pipe into the ground around the compost pile and bend in an inverted "U" shape. Set several of these hoops in a row. Lay plastic over the hoops and secure with bricks or staples made out of used coat hangers. Water generously and turn the pile several times as it cools to ensure a steady heat source. I have seen considerable heat generated from a 4' x 4' x 4' mound of shredded leaves activated with blood meal.

Another way to heat the bed with compost is dig a trench about two feet deep in late winter. Fill this trench with fresh, damp compost. Spread a two or three inch layer of soil over the compost. Plant the seedlings in the soil. Cover with the hoop cloche described above or a cold frame.

Summary
Propagating plants from seeds, tubers, rhizomes or bulbs is one of the most interesting and fascinating parts of horticulture. It reinforces our awareness of the change of seasons. It provides a great sense of accomplishment and brings us closer to the growing experience. Growing plants from seed offers both considerable savings and a greater variety of plants than are typically available locally.

The vast number of vegetable and herb varieties will provide activity and enjoyment for many years. As part of a comprehensive fitness lifestyle, propagating plants is yet another piece in the fitness puzzle.

Chapter Fourteen

Seasons

Dynamic gardening is not just a spring and summer activity. There are dozens of fall and winter activities that will keep your mind alert and your body active. You don't *have* to be exercising *in the garden* for an activity to be part of the Dynamic Gardening Way lifestyle.

Winter

Greenhouse/Indoor Gardening

Build a greenhouse to grow indoor plants during the winter months and start vegetables for spring planting. Greenhouses are available in a variety of shapes and priced from $100 to over $5,000. Commercial varieties range from inexpensive pop-up aluminum domes with plastic covering, to a medium size free-standing glass greenhouse with heating, lighting and ventilation. A list of greenhouses is in the Appendix.

A lean-to style greenhouse with a southern exposure connected to the back of the house is less costly than a free-standing greenhouse. You can use existing heating, electricity, and plumbing from the house.

A greenhouse is almost essential for growing difficult-flowering plants such as orchids, freesias, and cacti. A greenhouse increases gardening options significantly. When growing plants from seed, you can choose from a broader variety of plants than can be purchased locally. A greenhouse can provide virtually the entire garden with plants, saving hundreds of dollars annually over store-bought transplants, while providing many hours of pleasure, relaxation, and exercise during the cold winter months.

Some people associate greenhouses with *hydroponics*. Hydroponics is growing plants in water, without soil. Hydroponics uses moving water and a chemical nutrient solution to nourish plants grown in sand or pea gravel.

Hydroponics has been commercially successful for green leafy vegetables and tomatoes. While this is a fascinating and successful method of growing plants and vegetables it is actually the *opposite* of organic gardening which emphasizes the soil. However, many hydroponic organic gardeners use natural fish emulsion and kelp products in their water solution.

Absence from the Garden

Have you ever noticed how many fishing programs play on television in the dead of winter? Or, how, after a two-week vacation, you return to work revitalized and enthusiastic? How you miss the children after a few days away from them and even a "she hit me, dad!" doesn't sound all that bad?

Periods of high and low activity are normal. The midwinter's rest from the garden will increase your desire to garden in the spring. Ask any gardener during January as she pores through a stack of seed catalogs and a garden planner.

Seasonal Affective Disorder (SAD)

Recent research has shown that shorter days and reduced exposure to sunlight has an effect on our psychological health. *Seasonal Affective Disorder* (SAD) is a physiological response to reduced exposure to sunlight that causes depression in an estimated ten million Americans during fall and winter. Conversely, clinical studies have shown that exposure to intense, full-spectrum light can actually improve our moods. This is yet another reason why preparing the garden beds as the temperature warms up in early spring is so appealing.

Early spring

I highly recommend starting an early spring garden. Most of us need the exercise after a winter of relative inactivity. Another benefit is that insect pests are less plentiful in the early spring. This is particularly important to organic gardeners as well as gardeners in the South, where summer heat brings out insect pests in droves.

Start cool-weather brassicas, broccoli, cabbage, and cauliflower eight to ten weeks before the first frost date, and set out two to four weeks before the first frost date. Set transplants in a cold frame or protect with a row cover. Consult your local nursery, agricultural extension agent or a gardening neighbor to find out the best starting times in your area. Keep accurate seed-starting and planting records. They're indispensable to starting plants at the optimal time.

Move slow-growing perennials, started indoors during late winter, outside to a cold frame or protected area. Begin quick-growing tender annuals—marigolds, zinnia, celosia, coleus, and calendula—no sooner than three to five weeks before the last average frost date.

Gardening *extra* early requires:

1) Raised, well-drained garden beds.
2) Vegetable seeds or transplants.
3) Season extenders, such as Wall O' Waters™ (WOW) for tomatoes, a cold frame for hardening transplants, and row covers to protect plants from frost damage.

Wall O' Waters™ (WOW) are tepee-shaped, plant protectors with plastic sleeves which you fill with water. They are the only frost protection I've ever used that consistently protect tender annuals from freezing temperatures. They're best explained with an illustration:

Figure 14.1 Wall O' Water™ (WOW)

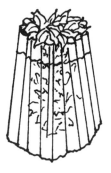

Spring planting

Cultivate the beds for planting by raking or tilling the soil surface. Remove rocks, sticks and other large items. Pulverize the soil with a tiller or hoe and rake smooth for planting. Cultivate the soil around plants by pulling weeds or cutting them off at the base with a hoe. Scratch the soil to prevent crusting.

When choosing plant location, be aware of *cross-pollination* which occurs when similar varieties are closely planted. Corn is most susceptible to cross-pollination; therefore, plant different varieties apart from one another. Squash varieties, zucchini and yellow squash, also cross-pollinate. It will not affect the taste and appearance of the vegetables but will affect the seeds.

After all threat of frost is past, plant tomatoes, peppers, eggplant, cucumbers, and squash. Wait until the soil warms up to plant melons and other heat-loving vegetables.

Weather

Pay careful attention to the first and last frost dates, soil dampness and soil temperature. Soil is too wet to work if a handful of dirt, when squeezed, packs tightly and does not crumble when released.

When the soil is too wet for planting, you can:

❀ Prune trees and bushes.
❀ Turn the compost pile.
❀ Cover the compost bin during the early spring rainy season. It may be damp but should drain quickly and be suitable for turning.
❀ Clean and prepare tomato cages and stakes.
❀ Cut trenches around perennial, herb and garden beds.
❀ Remove sod from new beds.

Another trick is to store extra soil, preferably sifted, in a shed, garage or under plastic where it will not get wet. This works particularly well with established beds that have loose, well-drained soil. Scratch the surface of the soil in the bed with a rake to clear away weeds. Sow radishes, spinach, lettuce or carrots, then cover with a fine layer of the dry, sifted soil. Sprinkle lightly with water.

Raised beds drain well. One rainy spring, I was able to prepare my beds after a three- to five-day break in the rain, whereas my conventional gardening neighbors had waterlogged gardens unworkable for four to six weeks.

Summer

Succession Planting

Follow a spring crop immediately with another that has a complementary feeding habit. Plant bush beans after spinach or lettuce; corn after peas; kale after melons.

Vegetables and Corresponding Exercise by Season

Season	Vegetable	Exercise
Spring	Lettuce Spinach Cabbage Broccoli Cauliflower Brussels sprouts ---------------- Swiss Chard Onions Herbs	Double dig garden beds Turn compost Spread compost in beds Rake beds Till larger areas Transplant perennials Sow seed
Summer	Tomatoes Cucumbers Peppers Eggplant Squash Bush beans Pole beans Corn Melons	Harvest Mulch Weed—standing: wide stance Weed—kneeling Cultivate Plant summer vegetables Circuit Training Mow lawn
Fall	Repeat first group of spring vegetables above Garlic Collards Turnip Greens Kale	Pull spent vegetables Sow cover crop/green manures Plant fall vegetables Cut/gather/store wood Prune bushes and trees Dig holes for trees

Crop Rotation

Alternate vegetable families each growing season. For example, rotate brassicas (cabbage, broccoli, cauliflower and Brussels sprouts) with beans; the solanaceae family (tomatoes, peppers, and eggplants) with legumes or green leafy vegetables (spinach, Swiss chard, collards, kale and turnip greens).

Mulching

Cover the ground around your plants with grass clippings, composted leaves, or wood chips. Mulching suppresses weeds, retains moisture and enriches the soil. Note that high carbon mulches can deplete nitrogen from the soil. Add a high nitrogen fertilizer such as blood or cottonseed meal before laying down a layer of aged wood chips or sawdust.

Drip Irrigation System

A soaker hose or perforated plastic tubing provides water to plant roots where they need it the most. If your climate has hot, dry months during the summer, a drip irrigation system can provide the necessary moisture to the plants while using less water. An automatic timer will ensure that the plants are receiving enough water. Vegetables should receive a minimum of one inch of water a week.

Fall

Fall vegetables are a repeat of spring vegetables with the addition of traditional fall crops: turnip greens, mustard greens, collards and kale. Growing vegetables in the fall extends both the harvesting and Dynamic Gardening Way exercise season. Use a layer of leaves, pine needles, row covers, or a cold frame to protect your plants from excessive cold.

Plant *green manures*: crimson clover, hairy vetch, cowpeas, and annual rye in the fall to add nitrogen and organic humus to the soil. Legumes fix nitrogen from the air on their nodules in the soil.

The principal role of a *cover crop* is protecting the ground from the effects of rain and wind: It reduces soil erosion, prevents soil compaction, aerates the soil and adds humus. Cover crops can also be green manures—the distinction is their primary purpose.

Divide and move lilies, daffodils, Jerusalem artichokes and the mint family in the fall. Plant leeks and elephant garlic and mulch heavily. The stalks will emerge in the early spring. Harvest the bulbs in June. Multiplier onions are an interesting variety of onion that produce small bulbs above the ground at the head of the stalk. Store these small bulbs and plant in the fall or early spring.

If you've started perennials from seed, move them outdoors in late summer/early fall. I currently move mine to a shaded area and protect them with a row cover during the winter. While a row cover does not protect as much as a clear plastic film, it allows air and water to reach the plants. In addition, two layers of a row cover create a "dead air space" that acts as an insulator against cold. In the early spring, I move them to a permanent location.

Late Fall

Keep busy with end of season maintenance activities: storing tomato cages, pulling spent vegetable plants, collecting leaves for compost, and pruning bushes and trees.

If you have plenty of trees, collect and compost leaves. Run over the leaves with a lawn mower or use a commercial *chipper/-shredder*.

I highly recommend a chipper/shredder. If you have a wooded lot, a source of leaves and plenty of spent vegetables you can create mounds of high-carbon material for the compost bin. The medium to large size models have two chutes: one for large materials, and another for chipping tree limbs. Usually twirling hammers shred the large materials and either one or two chipper blades chip the tree limbs. Medium and large models use 3.5, 5, and 8 horsepower, four-cycle, gasoline engines.

A medium-size chipper/shredder has a 5 horsepower engine and costs about $800. If this is too high for your budget, I recommend working with a neighborhood association, local garden club, or church to purchase one and share.

Smaller chipper/shredders are available with electric or two-cycle engines and have one chute. They are most often used for shredding small branches, leaves or spent garden vegetables.

Analyze your needs carefully before purchasing a chipper/-shredder. Some of the smaller models have very small chutes (for safety reasons) and shred leaves slowly. A large pile of leaves may take several hours. It may be quicker to spread the leaves out on the lawn and use a mulching lawn mower instead. Some leaf shredder models lay sideways on the ground and you can sweep the leaves into them.

While testing one model, we discovered that the fine grate would cause it to clog and jam often, particularly when materials were wet. After we installed the larger grate the leaves and tree limbs processed without a problem.

Determine the size of tree limbs you want to chip. Larger limbs might be better cut and used as kindling. The chipper blades tend to wear quickly when chipping hardwood limbs. Order an extra set and rotate them. Keep them sharp with an electric grinder wheel.

Be sure to purchase a chipper/shredder from a reputable dealer. Find out what the warranty, repair and return policy covers. We had trouble with one model that the company fixed twice at their expense without success. They ultimately sent a new machine. Later that year a metal bracket cracked and broke. Again, they replaced it at their expense.

Always wear goggles, gloves and a dust mask when using a chipper/shredder. The mask is especially important when shredding dry leaves. Don't wear any loose clothing or jewelry. Always use a stick or other object to push leaves, twigs and spent vegetables into the large chute.

Cleaning Tools

Late fall is an excellent time to clean and sharpen garden tools. This important maintenance activity burns calories and keeps the tools in top condition. All tools should be washed and wiped dry with a cloth. If they are rusted use steel wool or a wire brush on a drill to clean them. Paint the tools with a rust resistant enamel paint.

Use a file or a bench grinder to sharpen your shovels, hoes and weeders. If you use an electric grinder always wear goggles or protective glasses while sharpening tools. Also, sharpen the lawn mower blade. Sharp, clean tools cut more efficiently.

One handy trick is marking all tools with bright orange fluorescent tape or spray paint on the handle. There is nothing more difficult than finding brown-handled tools on brown dirt or brown grass in early spring.

Keeping Active

Remember, exercise doesn't always have to be strenuous to be beneficial. More than one weight-loss specialist I interviewed mentioned that *boredom* played a role in overeating. The wide variety of gardening activities are an extra health and weight-loss benefit. When you have nothing to do, it's easy to go to the refrigerator and snack.

Idleness can be your worst enemy. Transplanting and potting plants during the winter keep you active and off the couch. Even activities not directly related to gardening play a role in your environmentally-aware, healthy lifestyle. Cleaning up the tool shed, changing the spark plugs on the tiller and recycling aluminum cans are now part of your fitness regimen.

As winter returns and the seed catalogs pile high on your dinner table, you've come full circle. The gardening process continues.

Summary

Dynamic Gardening is a perfect example of the whole being more than the sum of its parts. Collecting seeds, saving aluminum cans or building a birdhouse are all part of your environmentally conscious, fitness lifestyle. Every facet of growing living things will help keep you fit and active through the change of seasons.

There is so much to learn, so much to experience, and so much to do, the success of the Dynamic Gardening Way lifestyle is measured in seasons, years and decades. The fruit trees, perennial vegetables, herbs and berry bushes, planted today, will yield delicious, nutritious herbs, fruits and vegetables three, five and ten years from now.

The Dynamic Gardening Way

Train to win with the understanding that the outcome is only part of the process of becoming a more complete human being, and does not define you as a winner or a loser.

Pay careful attention to gardening movements, stance and grip until correct form becomes an subconscious part of gardening.

*Do not **try** to be happy or relax, but allow yourself to become immersed in the moment, and experience the sights, sounds, smells, touch and taste sensations of the garden.*

Quick list of Do's and Don'ts for Beginning Dynamic Gardeners:

Do	Don't
Double dig and raise beds.	Use traditional rows except for corn and melons.
Create compost. Purchase or build a compost bin.	Use only commercial, bagged compost and topsoil mixes.
Shred leaves. Use in compost or as mulch.	Throw away leaves.
Save or mulch grass clippings. Use in compost.	Throw away grass clippings.
Build and enhance soil with organic amendments.	Rely on chemical fertilizers to grow plants.
Use organic fertilizers: blood, cottonseed and bone meal; fish emulsion, kelp and bat guano.	Use chemical fertilizers: ammonium nitrate, 13-13-13, herbicide and fertilizer mixes.
Use organic pesticides: Bt, pyrethrum, and rotenone.	Use chemical pesticides: Sevin™, malathion, diazinon, orthene and dursban.
Encourage beneficial insects: praying mantis, ladybugs and lacewing.	Apply broad-spectrum insecticides (chemical or organic) at the first sign of pests.
Use interplanting and companion planting.	Plant each variety by itself (called mono-cropping).
Plant spring and fall gardens	Plant only a summer garden.
Keep garden small and manageable.	Make garden too large.
Look at big picture of health and wellness	Worry excessively about chemical pesticides.

Chapter Fifteen

Fresh Fruits and Vegetables

More than ever, research emphasizes the importance of fresh fruits and vegetables in your diet. Leading health authorities advise cutting down on fat and increasing your intake of fiber-rich vegetables, fruits and grains. Vegetables contain dietary fiber, now viewed as critical to a balanced, healthy diet. Wheat grains, apple skins, and raw vegetables are excellent sources of dietary fiber. The Surgeon General's Report on Nutrition, and the Health National Research Council's study on diet and health conclude that Americans need to increase fiber intake and decease consumption of fat.

Using the garden to shape and change eating habits is an excellent way to increase fiber and reduce fat intake. Fruits and vegetables are packed with complex carbohydrates, vitamins and minerals, yet extremely low in fat. Vegetables such as cucumbers, green peppers, spinach, lettuce, celery and carrots have so few calories you can include an unlimited quantity in most diet programs.

The American Medical Association suggests that everyone should eat daily portions from the four basic food groups:

1) Dairy products   two to four portions
2) Meat, poultry & fish   two to four portions
3) Grains   four portions
4) Fruits and vegetables   four portions

Unfortunately, the American diet, once based on fresh fruits and vegetables, is now dominated by meat, processed foods and sugar-laden desserts and snacks. It's estimated that, on average, fat provides forty-two percent of the calories in the American diet. This is more than double the Recommended Daily Amount (RDA) of twenty percent. The National Cancer Institute recommends twenty to thirty grams of fiber each day. Americans eat, on average, only twelve to eighteen grams of fiber each day.

The grains, starches and vegetables of our forefathers' day have been replaced with meals loaded with excess protein, cholesterol and fat. In years past, we might have been able to eat all those extra fat calories without gaining weight. However, contemporary lifestyles are more sedentary and many don't exercise enough.

Complex carbohydrates, found in fresh fruits and vegetables, should account for up to fifty-five percent of the calories in your diet. The January, 1989 *American Journal of Clinical Nutrition* stated that, "Altering the composition of the diet in favor of a higher carbohydrate-to-fat ratio may decrease the incidence of obesity." Research has also shown that when participants switched to a diet high in complex carbohydrates, they became full more quickly, unconsciously decreasing their caloric intake.

The key to the success of the Dynamic Gardening Way is the superior taste, texture, and nutritional value of fresh fruits and vegetables. If the experts agree you should eat more fresh fruits and vegetables . . . .

Why not grow your own?

Really Fresh Food

You may have never eaten *really fresh* vegetables. Really fresh means picking red, juicy, home-grown tomatoes from your garden at 5:30 P.M., washing them, slicing them, and eating them for supper at 5:35 P.M.

And don't forget fresh sweet corn. Be sure to have the water boiling before you pick the corn. Fill the basket with fresh ears, shuck the ears as you walk into the house (don't trip over anything) and plunge them into the boiling water. After ten minutes, serve with a small pat of unsalted butter or margarine.

Saturday morning, pick strawberries for your cereal, and dill, chives, thyme and marjoram for your egg omelet. Grow herbs as close to your kitchen as possible, on a windowsill or a small 2' x 2' enclosure in your back yard. Anytime you want, fresh herbs are just steps away.

You can grow, for mere pennies, the same fresh fruits and vegetables served in *five-star restaurants*—leeks, French sorrel, yellow plum tomatoes, Merville Des Quatro Saisons loose-leaf lettuce, and finger-size carrots.

The higher quality of these savory delights will help you pass on the chips, doughnuts and pies for your snacks. Each tasty morsel will motivate you to maintain a daily "exercise" regimen of gardening. Each delicious bite will remind you to cultivate the garden beds, weed the vegetables and turn the compost pile.

Fresh Food Tastes Better

Compare a home-grown tomato, vine-ripened, juicy, and tart, to a rock-hard, flavorless, store-bought tomato. Chives, once started, return year after year and provide a delicious low-calorie seasoning for baked potatoes as well as beautiful lavender blossoms in early spring. New potatoes, freshly dug, are easy to grow and delicious. Fresh herbs, Swiss chard, corn, lettuce and spinach are noticeably different in taste, texture and nutrition to produce even a day or two old. The quality of the food we eat has been shown to play a role in our ability to lose weight.

Susan Schiffman, Ph.D., with the department of psychology at Duke University, notes, "The three things that have proven effective in reducing weight are: increasing exercise activity, reducing fat intake levels to twenty-five percent or less of total daily caloric intake, and keeping flavor levels of the food high."

The Dynamic Gardening Way meets all the objectives above with many additional benefits. Dr. Schiffman adds, "fresh food tastes better, but some *young people* are used to processed foods and actually prefer them. My daughter prefers frozen strawberries and concentrated orange juice over fresh strawberries and fresh squeezed orange juice."

I'm sure this is not an isolated case. Many youths have never seen a garden or experienced growing fresh fruits and vegetables. The problem is, as Dr. Garry, of the University of New Mexico, notes, "Many young people don't know how to garden." They've never had a chance to experience really fresh fruits and vegetables. This is why I emphasize introducing children, at the earliest age possible, to the pleasures of gardening.

Nutritional Components Higher

Your modern lifestyle may be hectic. Often you don't eat as well as you should. The typical response to potential vitamin or mineral deficiencies is to add vitamin and mineral supplements to your diet. Now, there's a new, long-term strategy: Optimize the nutritional value of the fruits and vegetables you eat by controlling variety, the soil in which they're grown and their freshness. Seven factors affect the nutritional quality of fruits and vegetables:

1) Variety

Advances in hybrids offer varieties of popular vegetables that contain more of certain vitamins. Vitamins are grouped into two general categories: fat-soluble vitamins—A, D, E and K; and water-soluble vitamins—C, and the eight B-complex vitamins.

The tomato varieties "Double-Rich" and "Sweet 100" contain more vitamin C than traditional varieties. "Butte Russet" Irish potatoes, Italian parsley and "Red Sails" lettuce contain more vitamin C than the more common varieties.

Beta carotene, found in vegetables and fruits, is a natural pigment that converts to vitamin A when metabolized by the digestive system. Carrots, hybrid tomatoes, sweet potatoes, green leafy vegetables, apricots, winter squash and cantaloupes are all excellent sources of beta carotene.

"A Plus" carrots, "Orange-Hi" spaghetti squash, "Golden Jersey" acorn squash, "Caro-Red" tomatoes, and "Jewel" sweet potatoes all contain more vitamin A than traditional varieties.

The "Dixie" butter pea is notably higher in calcium.

Jerusalem artichokes, a prolific cousin of the sunflower family, produce dozens of tasty water chestnut-like tubers high in vitamin B-1. Be sure to grow them in either pots or by themselves because the ground-running tubers will spread and take over a garden in a few years. (Believe me, I know. As my wife once asked me, "Jeff, what are these ten-foot sunflowers doing outside our kitchen window?")

These and many other varieties are available from the seed companies listed in the index of this book. Growing these high vitamin varieties from seed provides more nutritional punch for your gardening dollar.

2) Light
Exposure to light after picking decreases the amount of certain vitamins in vegetables, particularly riboflavin (B-2). Vitamin B-6 is stable to heat but sensitive to light. Light destroys vitamin K, found in green leafy vegetables.

3) Air (Oxidation)
Exposure to air reduces the amounts of B-complex vitamins found in green leafy vegetables: Swiss chard, spinach, collards, turnip greens and kale.

4) Heat
Melons, berries, tomatoes, cabbage, broccoli and green peppers contain vitamin C. The water-soluble vitamins, B-complex and C, are reduced when vegetables are boiled in water. Any type of cooking reduces both vitamin C and the B-complex vitamin content in food. Heat destroys folic acid, found in green leafy vegetables, fruit, and yeast. Potatoes are stripped of their vitamin C content when processed into instant mixes.

Magnesium, a mineral, is lost in commercial food processing as well as cooking water. Green leafy vegetables, a good source of magnesium, are best eaten raw.

5) Water (washing, soaking, canning and cooking)

Canning subjects food to the detrimental effects of both heat and water, with a devastating effect on the water-soluble vitamins. Thiamine and vitamin C are the most sensitive. Canning destroys 69% of thiamine, 64% of vitamin C, 61% of folate, and 55% of riboflavin. Soaking reduces the amounts of the water-soluble vitamins, C and B-complex, in fresh produce. Extensive washing, promoted as a way to remove potentially harmful pesticide residues, can wash valuable nutrients down the drain. Vegetables grown in a pesticide-free environment don't need extensive washing.

6) Storage

Some fruits and vegetables, especially those containing vitamin C, lose considerable nutrients just hours after picking. Extended storage and processing reduces levels of folic acid. Long storage, typical of produce shipped long distances, further reduces the nutritive value of fresh produce. Corn, for example, quickly converts sugar to starch after it's picked.

An interesting exception to the above is niacin, which is not destroyed by storage or heat. Niacin is found in peanuts and other legumes.

7) Soil Quality

Vegetables grown in soil deficient in a specific mineral will also be deficient. Adding a wide variety of organic materials helps balance nutrients. A soil test, usually available for a minor charge from your local agriculture extension agency is the best way to learn if a deficiency is present.

Trace elements: zinc, cobalt and selenium are commonly deficient in soil. They can be furnished though organic materials, such as seaweed and sea kelp.

Summary
Variety, light, air, heat, water, storage and soil quality all affect the vitamins and minerals in the food we eat. The traditional response is to purchase expensive vitamin and mineral supplements. I offer a new strategy: Increase the nutritional value of the food you eat. Grow your own.

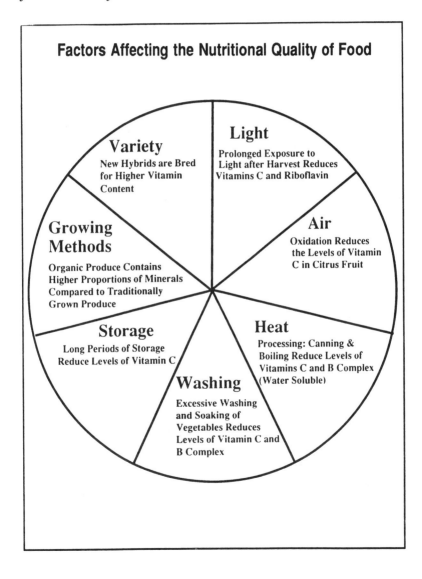

Factors Affecting the Nutritional Quality of Food

Variety
New Hybrids are Bred for Higher Vitamin Content

Light
Prolonged Exposure to Light after Harvest Reduces Vitamins C and Riboflavin

Growing Methods
Organic Produce Contains Higher Proportions of Minerals Compared to Traditionally Grown Produce

Air
Oxidation Reduces the Levels of Vitamin C in Citrus Fruit

Storage
Long Periods of Storage Reduce Levels of Vitamin C

Heat
Processing: Canning & Boiling Reduce Levels of Vitamins C and B Complex (Water Soluble)

Washing
Excessive Washing and Soaking of Vegetables Reduces Levels of Vitamin C and B Complex

Vegetables typically not available (at any price)

Many interesting and delicious vegetables are not available at any price, anywhere. Most of these hard-to-find taste treats either do not ship well, are expensive to grow, or have limited taste appeal. When these vegetables are available, the price is usually high and the quality low. This is because they don't "turn around" in the stores quickly—they may be several days old when you find them. Some of my favorite hard-to-find garden vegetables include:

Swiss chard

This hardy, three-season vegetable, is an excellent spinach substitute. More resistant to bolting (going to seed) than spinach, Swiss chard grows well in southern climates. The "Fordhook Giant" variety has enormous foot-long leaves which can be eaten raw or cooked like spinach. The long, thick stalks can be sliced and stir-fried with Chinese vegetables. The stalks of the red stemmed variety, Rhubarb chard, are tougher and more suited as an ornamental.

Malabar spinach

This attractive Southern spinach substitute grows on a red vine with thick, deep-green, heart-shaped leaves. It grows five or six feet up a trellis and provides tasty, nutritious greens all summer. Its many berry-like, black seed-pods self-sow.

"Chelsea" cherry tomatoes

This super-sweet cherry tomato is very similar to "Sweet One-hundred" but its fruit is twice as large or almost two inches in diameter. If you've never eaten a sweet cherry tomato, prepare for a treat. The plants grow seven feet tall and provide hundreds of cherry tomatoes all summer long. It is available from the Pinetree Seed Company listed in the Appendix.

Snow peas

While available in supermarkets and specialty shops, commercial snow peas are difficult to find at their peak of freshness. Snow peas are delicious and easy to grow. As a legume, they fix nitrogen from the air and enrich the soil. Taller varieties require a trellis for support. For those who don't wish to invest the time or money in trellises, several dwarf varieties are available. Grow them close together. They'll wrap around one another to a height of about eighteen inches.

Asparagus beans

Commonly known as "yard-long beans," these Oriental pole beans are prolific and yield tender beans that really do grow a yard long. They're best picked when twelve to eighteen inches long, deep green, shiny and pencil thick. Allow some to go to seed, and save some seeds each year to ensure a virtually inexhaustible supply of beans.

Armenian cucumber

This European cucumber has both an odd appearance and shape. The skin is light green and fluted. It has a habit of coiling around itself in a circular fashion and is best grown vertically on a trellis. The flavor is extremely mild, therefore it doesn't need peeling. The Armenian cucumber is particularly good marinated in salads or eaten raw with a dip.

Elephant Garlic

Elephant garlic is milder and much larger than ordinary garlic. Plant garlic bulbs in the fall and mulch heavily. Harvest and divide each year in late spring after the stalks turn yellow. Don't allow elephant garlic to flower as it reduces the size of the bulb. When the flower blossoms form, cut them off. An initial planting of a dozen bulbs yields about three dozen or more garlic bulbs the following year. From the harvest, eat about half, save the other half for next season. Continue this sequence each year. Result: an inexhaustible supply of garlic available for cooking—essentially free!

Kale

More often grown in the North than the South, this underrated and often ignored vegetable is actually the most nutritious of all. It contains high proportions of vitamins A, C, calcium, iron and potassium. It's a sad fact that, more often than not, kale is never eaten but served as a garnish. It certainly deserves a better fate. Kale is easy to grow and tolerates both heat and cold. In fact, a light frost actually improves the flavor.

Edible Flowers

Flowers of chives (*Allium schoenoprasum* and *A. tuberosum*), borage (*Borago officinalis*), nasturtium (*Tropaeolum majus*), pinks (*Dianthus spp.*), bee balm (*Monarda didyma*), and calendula (*Calendula officinalis*) are all edible. Botanical names are indicated for edible flowers, because it's important to know exactly what you're eating. Common names vary and may include several different plants, some of which may be poisonous.

Herbs

Herbs are invaluable as a means to add flavor and zest to meals without the addition of salt, butter, cream sauces and condiments. A windowsill garden of basil, sweet marjoram, dill, chives, sage and thyme will provide herbs all year, both fresh and dried. Perennial herbs: sage, oregano, thyme, and winter savory, once established, will return year after year. Growing your own offers significant savings over store bought.

Varro Tyler, Ph.D., author of *The Honest Herbal*, and an expert in the therapeutic use of herbs, supports the use of fresh herbs versus dried. He notes that "many herbs have volatile oils that evaporate when dried and stored."

Several herbs have been clinically proven to have medicinal benefits. Garlic can lower cholesterol. Peppermint oil aids digestion. Catnip tea is beneficial for its calming effect on humans, the opposite influence it has on cats.

Herbal teas are widely used in diets. An entire weight loss industry has been formed on the premise that herbal teas aid the weight loss process. Dr. Tyler notes, "No single herb has been shown to be effective as a diet aid. Herbs used in commercial weight loss programs are actually laxatives or diuretics." (Which, with continued use, can cause potassium and magnesium deficiencies.)

Growing herbs is one of the more interesting subsets of gardening. The variety of herbs is almost endless. A few plants provide seasoning for dozens of meals and they are well suited for small space gardens.

Most cities have active herb societies. Also, your local botanical gardens may have demonstration gardens that feature ornamental, culinary and therapeutic herbs.

Highly Nutritious Vegetables, Legumes and Seeds

Several other vegetables and flowers, typically not grown in the home vegetable garden, are highly nutritious.

Sunflowers

These easy to grow, impressive looking flowers have several functions in the garden. The seeds are a good source of protein, the stalks go into the compost pile, and the tall plants can be a border or accent point in the flower garden. Sunflower roots emit a substance which inhibits plant growth, therefore it's best to plant them away from the main garden beds.

Edible soybeans

Edible soybeans are a nitrogen-fixing legume that will benefit any other vegetable they're grown near in the garden. Certain varieties are grown to be eaten while still green. Grow soybeans like any other bean, and harvest while still green for a protein packed snack or as part of a main course. Soybeans like hot weather and do well in the South. They're available from Johnny's Selected Seeds and others.

Sesame

This drought-tolerant, tender annual has attractive purple-white flowers and does well in the South and Southwest. It should be planted after all danger of frost is past. Collect the seeds and use in baking, or add to vegetables and casseroles. Seeds contain lecithin and vitamin E.

Peanuts

Although I've never grown peanuts, those with a suitably warm climate (120 frost-free days) might try this interesting plant. Peanuts are actually a legume. They require loose, friable soil because the stems sprawl on the soil where the spent flowers grow downward into the soil and develop into the peanut pod.

Pesticides and the Food We Eat

Although I personally don't use any chemical pesticides on the fruits and vegetables I grow, I don't worry about chemical pesticides on the food I buy. Surprised? Broad-spectrum, persistent pesticides are harmful to beneficial insect populations and the environment. *Excessive* pesticide residues can be harmful to humans. From a *fitness perspective*, however, the *big picture* is moderate exercise, sound nutrition and psychological well-being. The key word in nutrition is *variety and balance*. Eating a well-balanced diet of fruits, vegetables, grains, dairy products and fish or meat products is still the best strategy to good health.

Dr. Bruce Ames, a genetic toxicologist and professor of biochemistry and molecular biology at the University of California at Berkeley, developed a test for finding potential cancer–causing agents back in the 1970s, and, for several years, was the darling of the environmental movement. In his writings, Dr. Ames notes:

"Epidemiologists try to discover the causes of cancer by studying people. They have been pretty successful at figuring out that cigarette smoking causes cancer and diet has a big influence on cancer, as do viruses."

In an interview with Dr. Ames, he said:

"Home grown fruits and vegetables taste better and Americans don't eat enough fruits and vegetables for health. Americans aren't exercising enough and gardening is wonderful exercise. So many people reluctantly jog and exercise on weekends when gardening can provide exercise with greater satisfaction. My wife and I garden all the time.

"Recent research indicates that only nine percent of the American public is eating the recommended amount of fruits and vegetables a day. Yet, recent research shows that in 89 out of 99 studies, diet was directly attributed to health."

An interesting fact is that there are *natural carcinogens* (cancer-causing substances) in plants. Plants create their own toxins to fend off predators. Fortunately, humans have many defenses against both natural and chemical carcinogens. Dr. Ames further adds:

"The good things about eating fruits and vegetables far outweigh any concern over potential harmful residues. You ingest more natural carcinogens from a single cup of coffee than the chemical residues you'll ingest from eating commercially grown fruits and vegetables all year."

I include this information to make two points: one, that fear of pesticides need not be your *main reason* for using sustainable and organic gardening techniques. The exercise, environmental and savings benefits should be reason enough. The second point is that the subject of carcinogens is complex—exceedingly complex. As an example, Dr. Ames adds:

"Of all dietary pesticides, 99.99% are natural: there are toxins produced by plants to defend themselves against fungi, insects, and other animal predators. Because each plant produces a different array of toxins, we estimate that, on average, Americans ingest roughly 5,000 to 10,000 different natural pesticides and their breakdown products. We also estimate that Americans eat about 1,500 milligrams of natural pesticides per day, which is 10,000 times more than they consume of synthetic pesticide residues."

Before you decide to stop eating all together, there is good news. Dr. Ames concludes:

"Epidemiologists have gathered extensive evidence that a major risk factor for heart disease and cancer is insufficient consumption of vegetables. Surveys indicate that 90% of the U.S. population does not eat enough fruits and vegetables for optimal health (Patterson and Block, 1991). The various defenses to combat degenerative biochemical processes that occur in normal metabolism depend on micronutrients. The micronutrients in fruits and vegetables, particularly the antioxidants (vitamin C, vitamin E, and beta-carotene) and folic acid, are known to prevent disease; and many other vitamins and minerals may be important as well.

". . . eating sufficient amounts of fruits and vegetables (about 5 servings per day) is one of the best preventive measures against cancer and other degenerative diseases . . . "

Antioxidants

The *free radical hypothesis* of aging is receiving increased attention from the medical community. Free radicals result from oxidation in our bodies. When an organic compound (any compound containing carbon) reacts with an oxygen molecule, a free electron is released damaging healthy cells, which many believe to be the chief cause of aging.

Antioxidants, vitamins E, C and beta-carotene, inhibit this process. Eating fruits and vegetables high in antioxidants should always be your first line of defense. The body converts beta-carotene to vitamin A in the body, however, vitamin A is not an antioxidant. A low-fat diet may be low in fat–soluble vitamins, particularly vitamin E, therefore, a vitamin supplement may be warranted.

The anti-aging industry, now estimated at $2-billion a year, is rife with questionable cures, megadose vitamin supplements and miracle anti-aging formulas. Ironically, the best solution is both simple and inexpensive. The medical consultants at *Consumer Reports*, in the January, 1992 edition, recommend, "eating a well-balanced, low-fat, high-carbohydrate diet, exercising regularly, refraining from smoking and alcohol abuse, and avoiding obesity" as the *best* strategy to maximize your longevity. Once again, a healthy lifestyle, not fad cures or gimmicks, is the best wellness strategy.

The following fruits, nuts, oils and vegetables are high in antioxidants.

Vitamin C	Beta-Carotene	Vitamin E
Hot peppers	Carrots	Soybean oil
Sweet peppers	Sweet potatoes	Sunflower seeds
Kale	Kale	Corn oil
Broccoli	Butternut squash	Almonds
Cauliflower	Turnip greens	Peanuts (roasted)
Mustard	Spinach	Sesame seeds
Kohlrabi	Hubbard squash	Wheat germ
Snow peas	Mustard	Walnuts
Turnip greens	Collards	Pecans
Cabbage	Cantaloupe	Pumpkin seeds
Cantaloupe	Leaf lettuce	Brown rice
Asparagus	Pumpkins	Rye
English peas	Broccoli	Barley
Spinach	Chinese cabbage	Green leafy vegetables
Chinese cabbage	Tomatoes	

Sources for chart: *Gardening for Nutrition*, University of Tennessee Agricultural Extension Service, PB 1228-5M-12/87. Burtis, Grace, Ph.D., R.D., Davis, Judi, M.S. R.D., and Martin, Sandra, R.N., *Applied Nutrition and Diet Therapy*, W.B. Saunders Company, Philadelphia PA, 1988.

Summary

One objective of the Dynamic Gardening Way is to increase the convenience, quantity, appeal and nutritional value of fresh fruits and vegetables—the naturally healthy foods that so often are *not* a part of your diet. The taste of *really* fresh vegetables is a treat many have never experienced.

The Dynamic Gardening Way

Every day, learn to change those events/actions you can (soil, pest management, varieties) and not worry about those you cannot (weather, seasons, poor seed).

Garden, not to impress others with the size of your harvest or how hard you work, but for the spontaneous enjoyment of your awareness.

Fitness is not a Varsity letter or championship ring, but moderate exercise, a sound diet and psychological wellbeing.

Never view exercise or fruits and vegetables as a sacrifice you must endure to attain your goal of living a long, healthy life—learn to enjoy every moment along the way.

Chapter Sixteen

Proper Preparation

Yes, there are overweight gardeners and farmers. Heredity, metabolism, and body type all play a role in how you process calories. While there is little you can do about heredity or body type, you can control how you *prepare* the food you eat. The primary culprit for weight gain may not be lack of exercise or eating the wrong foods but adding butter, heavy sauces, sour cream and salt to naturally low-calorie fruits and vegetables. Fruits and vegetables are most nutritious when they're processed the least. The concept of "convenience food" takes on new meaning when you grow your own.

Eat Vegetables Uncooked

This ranks high on the nutrition and convenience scales. Raw spring and fall vegetables: lettuce, spinach, snow peas, radishes, cauliflower and broccoli provide a quick salad for lunch or dinner. Add a little vinaigrette made with fresh onion, garlic, parsley, oregano, marjoram, thyme and chives from the herb garden.

During the summer, raw zucchini, summer squash, peppers, tomatoes, and cucumbers make a nutritious, low-calorie snack. They're delicious mixed in a salad with fresh herbs, oil and vinegar or with a yogurt-based dip.

Juicing

Juicing vegetables in a blender or juice extractor is a nutritious and convenient way to prepare fresh produce. Fresh tomatoes, celery, carrots and an apple (for sweetness) make a refreshing vegetable cocktail noticeably different from the pasteurized commercial variety. Fresh strawberries, blueberries, or raspberries make a delicious shake juiced and blended with crushed ice or skim milk.

Steam Rather Than Boil

Steaming broccoli, cauliflower, carrots, and green beans reduces the amount of water-soluble vitamins lost during the boiling process. Steaming also keeps them fresh and crisp.

Microwave Foods

Microwaving fresh vegetables is a quick and convenient way to cook vegetables while preserving their taste and crispness. Eggplant, typically fried, soaks up oil adding numerous calories to a naturally low-calorie vegetable. Try microwaving eggplant in a covered dish with fresh herbs, squash, onions and mushrooms.

Broil and Bake

Whenever possible, broil or bake vegetables, meat and fish. Combine cabbage, zucchini, tomatoes, onions and peppers in aluminum foil, and bake over a charcoal fire for a delightful summer treat.

Use Fresh Herbs Instead of Salt

Substitute a fresh herb mixture for salt on vegetables, meats, fish, and eggs. Chives, parsley, marjoram, basil, dill, and sage add lots of flavor and few calories. Several herb plants can provide seasonings, both fresh and dried, all year.

Avoid Deep-Frying

Deep-frying is probably one of the major reasons gardeners and farmers are overweight. Frying is popular because it enhances the taste of foods. If you feel you can't eliminate fried foods completely, at the very least cut down on the frequency and quantity of fried foods you eat.

Stir-Fry

Instead of deep-frying, stir-fry vegetables quickly at a high temperature. Garden vegetables retain their flavor and crispness when stir-fried.

Avoid Fatty Sauces, Creams and Condiments

Mayonnaise, butter, margarine, and cream sauces are mostly empty fat calories. Don't be mislead by the fact that margarine and vegetable oil are cholesterol-free, that they don't contain fat. They're *all* fat. Canola, safflower and sunflower oil are lowest in *saturated fat*, which is the most harmful. Other types of fat, monounsaturated and polyunsaturated, don't pose the same health hazards but still add empty calories to your diet.

Summary

The conventional wisdom is that most physicians, nutritionists, and health specialists don't want you to eat anything that tastes good. That's not true when you grow your own fruits and vegetables. It's no longer necessary to mask the flavor of fruits and vegetables with butter, salt and fat and sugar-laden condiments.

In a society where packaged and processed foods are inexpensive and convenient it takes time to recondition your taste buds to appreciate fresh, whole foods. Enjoy the natural goodness of your harvest with simple, nutritious preparation.

Chapter Seventeen

Beyond Diet and Exercise

You might eat a sensible diet, consuming adequate portions from the four main food groups each day. You prepare the food without adding unnecessary calories, and you exercise at least twenty minutes every day. The pounds are dropping at a slow but steady rate of about one to two pounds a week. Everything is going well.

And then you quit. You binge on pizza and beer with friends. You've had a "bad day" at the office and consume an entire bag of potato chips. The children are fighting, and you can't get them to behave. Later that night, you consume half a blueberry pie. Far fetched? Not really.

A proper diet and exercise program will not succeed if psychological factors are not addressed. Many begin diets and exercise programs with enthusiasm and good intentions, only to quit after a few weeks or months. This yo-yo syndrome of losing weight and regaining is commonplace and adds to feelings of failure and inadequacy.

There are other, more serious reactions to weight loss. *Bulimia*—binge eating followed by purging, is an increasingly common eating disorder. Many bulimics excessively use diuretics and laxatives.

Anorexia nervosa is a psychological condition where people virtually stop eating until the person is emaciated and weak. In spite of their condition, they continue to think they're still fat as they waste away to nothing.

While psychologists wrestle with the causes of these severe eating disorders, millions of dieters and exercise enthusiasts simply stop for any one of a hundred reasons. Maintaining a healthy weight and exercising over a lifetime is more complicated than reading a book and following a step-by-step diet program the rest of our lives. We're not computers that can be programmed to run flawlessly for years—even though most diet and exercise programs act as if we were. Even the experts are divided over the causes for our unpredictable eating behaviors.

The two schools of thought on eating disorders differentiate between symptoms from *psychological causes* and *physiological responses* to perceived starvation. One school views eating disorders as symptoms of underlying *psychological* causes: childhood trauma, sexual abuse, low self-esteem, and stress. Many patients with eating disorders have one or more of these psychological problems.

I don't propose that gardening can cure or help someone with an eating disorder that is the result of underlying psychological causes. Anyone who has an eating disorder should see an appropriate health-care professional.

The other school, based on recent research, views starving and binging habits as a *physiological response* to food deprivation. When your body feels it's being starved, it responds by conserving energy and releasing chemicals in the brain that trigger defense mechanisms. The rate of weight loss stops. Your body craves food. This explanation is most applicable to the behaviors of "Starvers, Stuffers and Skippers" as outlined in Dr. Callaway's book.

Related to the above physiological theory is the "set point" theory, which suggests that your body has a genetically determined set point—a level of fat that is appropriate for your body type and age. When you deviate from this set point, your body resists. Research has shown that normal weight individuals stop eating sweetened or fatty foods sooner than obese persons. The best way to lower the set point is through physical exercise and increasing muscle mass.

The physiological explanation is particularly important when comparing the gardening lifestyle to artificial and short-term diet programs. It points out the flaw of quick weight-loss programs. The media, weight-loss clinics and most people want fast, impressive results. But quick weight-loss is not in your long-term interest. The probability is higher than ninety percent that you will gain the weight back. The fact that you're focused on *gardening* and not *dieting* or *exercising* may be the most significant ingredient to the success of the Dynamic Gardening Way.

If you're dieting problems fall in the less serious areas of lapsed exercise, snacking, skipping meals and occasional binging, I suggest getting out of the dieting mentality. Don't focus on the diet—focus on a healthy lifestyle. The experts will be debating the causes of weight gain for years to come. In the meantime you want to get off the diet-and-exercise roller coaster and enjoy your life. The dynamic gardening lifestyle can help you in three ways.

First, gardening is an "outward directed" activity. In other words, you plant seeds, cultivate the soil, double dig beds and turn the compost pile with the goal of growing fruits and vegetables to eat. These tasks occupy your mind and exercise your body. Focusing on the task at hand and away from ourselves is an important step in eliminating debilitating "self-talk" and behaviors. Simply put, while you're weeding the pepper plants, you shouldn't be worrying about "Does Terry like me?" "What will happen if this plant doesn't grow?" or "How much do I weigh today?"

Second, gardening promotes a healthy lifestyle you can enjoy for a lifetime. Growing plants is personally rewarding. There is always some gardening activity, no matter how small, that can enrich your life.

Third, gardening lets *you* be *you*. Most experts note that if you're twenty-five percent over your ideal weight and it's not muscle mass, then the extra weight is a health concern. However, if your body type favors a set point weight of 150 pounds instead of 130 and you're comfortable at that weight don't let others dictate your image of yourself. Find *new friends*. Join a local gardening association, or start one if there isn't any in your town. Join a wilderness preservation society or other environmental organization. Start a community composting or youth gardening program. You'll meet people with common interests that go beyond the superficial.

The ideas in this book transcend common perceptions and rules of health and fitness. Just because someone looks healthy doesn't mean he/she is. While the health experts advise you to change your image of what's attractive, the media won't let you forget. Where can you find others who are interested more about what they do than what they wear? Where can you find others who are concerned about the environment? Where can you find others who are caring and nurturing? Where can you find others who are healthy and fit? Try the universe of gardeners. You'll meet some great people.

Summary
The "Role of the Mind" cannot be ignored. For serious eating disorders see a qualified specialist. However, gardening can be an important tool in your quest for physical and psychological fitness. The most important factor is developing a positive, "can do" attitude. The next chapter explores how to overcome misconceptions about gardening and turn obstacles into challenges.

How to get gardening on a television talkshow.

Chapter Eighteen

Sounds Interesting, But . . . .

I've included this chapter in the psychology section because I feel that if we really want something, we'll overcome any obstacle set before us. If you're new to gardening, adopting the lifestyle is not going to be quick or easy. It's not a no-effort, one-time solution to all your weight and health problems. *Fitness the Dynamic Gardening Way* will change how you view gardening forever. It's a health and wellness plan for the rest of your life.

This chapter is for those who are always thinking of reasons something won't work. When I was president of the Mid-South Organic Network, a volunteer association dedicated to promoting organic gardening, I always heard dozens of excuses why someone could not or would not garden. Usually, I could suggest a solution to any obstacle.

Then, someone would ask, "What about . . . an Eskimo, floating on an ice block . . . in the ocean. How does *he* garden?" You win. I'm stumped. I agree, this book isn't for everybody. If you're thinking that way, *you're missing the whole point!*

Anyone can think of reasons something *won't* work. It takes a *unique* individual to overcome obstacles and achieve a personal goal. I'm often asked whether this is an exercise book, a diet book or a gardening book. It's really all three. I'll even add another element. It's a *motivational* book. After reading this book, I want you to jump off the couch and begin a new fitness program—dynamic gardening.

I want to motivate you to try something new, something different: stepping up on a box between weeding the petunia beds; walking around the garden in leg weights while pruning roses; and raking, hoeing and digging with an exaggerated, legs apart, back straight, knees bent stance.

I don't expect everyone to follow *all* the ideas outlined in this book. The Dynamic Gardening Way is not an all or nothing proposition. It's a flexible program you can modify to suit your personal needs. Remember, no one is keeping score, and there are no referees. You may exercise as much or as little as you like.

Perhaps you travel frequently, have a small backyard, or work until after dark. The following pages offer ideas and suggestions on how to overcome many common gardening (and fitness) obstacles and achieve your health and gardening objectives. Problems now become "challenges."

"Just don't have the time"

The most common excuse I hear is, "Well, that's not a bad idea, but I just don't have the time to garden." I propose that:

Gardening Saves Time

Current Activity	Gardening Alternative	Time Saved
Drive to supermarket, select food, pay and drive home.	Walk to back yard, pick produce, walk to house.	20 minutes
Drive to a fast-food outlet, purchase food, pay, eat and going home.	Same as above.	20 minutes
Drive to health spa or aerobic class, work out and drive home.	Walk to back yard, dig garden beds, turn compost, weed or cultivate.	1 hour
Cycle, jog, power-walk, do aerobics or other exercise to keep fit.	Substitute equal amount of back yard gardening exercise and Circuit-Training.	1 hour
Set aside time to spend with children.	Garden with children in back yard.	1 hour
Sunbathe in back yard or local pool.	Garden while wearing bathing suit.	2 hours
Cut coupons to save on grocery bills.	Growing fruits and vegetables saves money.	20 minutes
Relax and listen to music.	Listen to music while gardening.	2 hours
Relax and smell the roses.	You're already doing this!	As much as you want!

Dispelling Stereotypes

"I don't have a green thumb."

I hear this about as often as "I don't have the time." Many psychological theories explain how, as children we believe as fact the opinions of our peers and parents. Those around us shape our thoughts and feelings about ourselves. These self-images are formed early and remain with us into adult life even after we've outgrown our perceived "flaws."

Our thoughts shape our behavior as strongly as any external stimulus. If we believe we're poor gardeners, when we grow ten plants and five die, half the plants *died*, and we feel we've failed. If we believe we're good gardeners, when five plants die, half the plants *lived*, and we plant five more.

A number of books, such as Dr. Harris' *I'm Okay, You're Okay*, Albert Ellis' *Guide to Irrational Living*, and Dr. Wayne Dwyer's *Erroneous Zones*, describe this idea in more detail. While they each have their own name for the phenomenon, it's essentially the same—our thoughts about ourselves influence how we perceive the world.

We're most comfortable when our external reality conforms to our image of ourselves. If we believe we can achieve straight A's, we can. If we believe we can score the winning touchdown, we can. If we believe we can grow anything, we can. Conversely, if we believe we can't grow anything, then we'll succeed—to *not* grow anything.

Each year, I lose dozens of plants, maybe hundreds. For any number of reasons, they shrivel and die. But I grow *so many* I always have more ready to take their place. Everyone says I have a green thumb. I'm just persistent. My wins outnumber my losses.

Take a moment and reflect on how gardening makes you feel. Ask yourself, "What am I telling myself?" If you're telling yourself negative thoughts, I recommend the relaxation techniques and the "self-talk" exercises I describe in chapter 21.

Find out what successful gardeners do. More importantly, *learn how they think.* Talk to successful gardeners in your neighborhood. Join a gardening association. Volunteer at the local botanical garden or nature center.

There's no such thing as a green thumb. Some gardeners may be better than others, but anyone can improve by reading, asking questions, and experimenting.

Gardening does require a level of consistency. This is where most people fail. You do need to tend the garden periodically. Vegetables need about an inch of water a week. Harvest the vegetables every day or two during peak harvest season. You need to pull weeds to reduce insect pests and competition for nutrients.

Some plants are better suited to your climate and soil than others. For years, I've tried to grow blueberry bushes. Each year, they grow a little and produce a few more blueberries than the year before. They grow—they just don't flourish. Last year, a friend gave me some black raspberries. This plant fits my personal needs profile: fast growing, tolerates neglect, and a generous producer.

Starting plants from seed is another problem for many people. It's simply a matter of having the *right tools.* The Accelerated Propagation System, described earlier, transformed me, virtually overnight, from a frustrated gardener to one who felt he could grow *anything* from seed.

A green thumb is little more than:

- ❀ Having a positive attitude
- ❀ Doing simple things well
- ❀ Counting successes, not failures
- ❀ Learning from your mistakes
- ❀ Having the right tools
- ❀ Matching plants to your climate
- ❀ Matching gardening goals to your lifestyle
- ❀ Being persistent

Don't sell yourself short. *You, too* can have a green thumb. You only have to believe in yourself.

Too Much Shade

Many fruits and vegetables require at least six hours of sun each day. However, lettuce, spinach and Swiss chard are shade tolerant. Many herbs—thyme, parsley, rue, sage, rosemary and marjoram—will tolerate some shade.

Try woodland wildflowers that normally grow under trees and need only minimal light. They also require very little care once established. Growing hundreds of woodland plants will produce a stunning display of colors and fragrances. Shade loving perennial plants include hardy ferns, hostas, columbine (Aquilegia), lobelia, and astilbe.

Wildflower associations often work with local developers to remove native wildflowers before the bulldozers arrive. To those of us with an abhorrence of "waste," this is a particularly gratifying activity.

If you crave tomatoes, peppers, squash and other sun-loving vegetables then look around your neighborhood for a suitable location and start a community garden.

Not Enough Daylight

Three more reasons why you cannot garden:

1) "There is not enough daylight after I come home from work to enjoy outdoor activities."
2) "I'm a night person."
3) "It's too hot in the summer to garden."

Sound familiar? Personally, these really hit home. I'm a night person who loves gardening. My peak performance is typically between ten and two o'clock—at night! During the summertime, I enjoy swimming with my family after work, between six and eight o'clock. That cuts down on my harvesting, weeding, mulching and cultivating exercises.

To solve these problems, I set up two, twin-bulb, 150-watt floodlights in my garden. They provide enough light to harvest, weed, cultivate and mulch the garden. An inexpensive alternative is to purchase a portable, rechargeable fluorescent light.

I've turned the compost pile at ten o'clock at night. I've double dug garden beds at midnight. It's cooler at night and gardening didn't interfere with my children's swimming, an activity they love.

Frequent Traveling

Many who travel often feel they can't garden because they're away from home too much. Traveling as much as three to five days a week, every week, should not prevent you from reaping the diet and exercise benefits of gardening. Follow these steps, and you can have a successful garden.

Your main goal should be creating an optimal growing environment for the plants. I recommend deep-dug, raised beds for optimal root penetration, soil aeration, and moisture retention. This promotes strong, healthy plants. A broader root system can withstand drought. In addition, vegetables can be planted three times closer in this ultra-fertile environment. Closer spacing shades the ground between plants reducing weed growth. If your area has long periods of dry weather, try using a soaker-hose irrigation system with an automatic timer.

Someone in your family could help with the garden while you're away. Garden with a neighbor who would be willing to inspect, pick, and spray the vegetables while you're absent. Hire one of the neighbor's children to pick and tend plants.

Purchase a mini-tiller. Use it to prepare small garden areas, spot-weed between beds and paths or mix fresh compost into the soil. It can shorten three hours of exercise to forty minutes or less. Just having a mini-tiller available provides peace of mind. When you have the time and need the exercise, maintain the garden manually. When you need to meet your friends on the golf course—use a mini-tiller.

Vacations

I'll assume a two week vacation. Preparation is similar to frequent travel with the following additional advice:

- ❀ Pick nearly everything before you leave, even if it's small. Pick all tomatoes with even a hint of orange.
- ❀ If you don't have an automatic timer and irrigation system, soak the garden thoroughly—several inches deep.
- ❀ Have a neighbor pick vegetables and check for insect pests while you're gone.
- ❀ Weed thoroughly before you leave. Lay down black plastic on weed-prone areas.
- ❀ Mulch heavily around plants with wood chips, grass clippings, and shredded newspaper.
- ❀ Lay down temporary transportable mats, cut from discarded carpeting or cardboard between plants to reduce weed growth.
- ❀ If you plan to be away from the garden frequently for weeks at a time, in the spring, lay down black plastic over most of the garden to prevent weed growth. This works well for peppers, tomatoes, squash, eggplant and all melons. Punch holes in the plastic to allow drainage. Set a brick or other support under any ripening melon. It will rot if it sits in water on the plastic under the hot sun.

Geography or Climate Not Suitable

There are regional challenges. Some areas, notably California, have been plagued by drought. The Northeast and upper Midwest have short growing seasons and cold winters. The South has hot summer temperatures, high humidity and hard clay soil.

If drought is a problem, I recommend *sunken* versus raised beds. Sunken beds have earthen walls that contain water and concentrate it toward the plants. A drip irrigation hose, sunk six inches beneath the soil, will provide moisture to the plants at the root level with minimal evaporation or runoff.

In the Deep South, gardening can be enjoyed nearly all year. The worst time is during the intense heat of midsummer. Wind down gardening activities when the daytime temperature reaches the mid-90s. Garden only in the early morning, late afternoon, or at night using lights. Concentrate on varieties that tolerate drought, heat and humidity. Hastings Seeds, listed in the Appendix, offers an excellent selection of Southern vegetables, fruit trees, berry bushes and perennials.

Heavy Clay Soil

My current garden was once solid clay. While clay soil has drawbacks for gardening, it's a plus for exercising. Improving heavy clay soil and "hardpan" to friable loam is a long-term project. The key to improving poor soil is lots of organic matter. Have your clay soil tested and if it's acidic add lime and wood ashes.

I also recommend adding "soil conditioners." One is gypsum (hydrous calcium sulfate) which helps break up clay soil. Nitron Formula A-35™, (Nitron Industries), and ROOTS™, (Gardener's Supply Company) are not fertilizers in the traditional sense, but improve the soil by providing enzymes that help break down organic matter and increase the friability of the soil.

Colder Regions of Northeast and Midwest

The short growing seasons of colder regions offer challenges as well as benefits. For one, the summers are usually mild, providing an optimal climate for moderate to heavy exercise in the garden.

Lengthen the short growing season by using the season extenders discussed earlier: row covers, cold frames, Wall-O'-Waters, hot beds, indoor lights or a greenhouse.

Typically, soils west of the Mississippi are alkaline: therefore, acidic materials, cottonseed meal and leaves are good organic amendments to lower the pH.

Not Enough Space

Small container gardens have been established in planters and pots on the rooftops of buildings in many major urban areas. A small garden, 10' x 10', using intensive techniques, can yield bushels full of vegetables and herbs. Establish a windowsill garden and planters if you don't have much outdoor space.

Use bottomless pots around a patio to grow herbs, lettuce, pixie tomatoes and pepper plants. The one, two and five gallon plastic containers that nurseries use for large plants and bushes are ideal. Use a shears or sharp knife to cut out the bottom and sink them two-thirds of the way into the ground. Carrots, garlic, onions, radishes, lettuce and spinach are excellent small space vegetables. If you have a south-facing wall grow cucumbers and peas or beans up a trellis from a one or two foot open-bottom planter.

Establish a community garden or volunteer to work with the local Botanic Gardens. Even a small garden will have exercise, nutritional and, most importantly, psychological benefits. Add Circuit Training and cross-training to your exercise regimen.

Summary

Whether it's heat, cold, drought, wind or pestilence, obstacles are always in your way to a successful garden. Most can be overcome with planning, a few tricks and the correct mental attitude. The next chapter discusses how gardening can be used as a tool to reduce stress.

Chapter Nineteen

Stress

If asked, gardeners will talk for hours about how growing plants helps them unwind at the end of a long day at work. Wearing old clothes and getting dirty, working at a steady but unhurried pace, taking control of their environment, and exercising are all conducive to relaxing mind, body and spirit.

However, to infer that gardening is intrinsically relaxing is incorrect. It's how we *approach* gardening that calms us. When our body and mind are focused on a task, we're relaxed. If we view gardening as a chore, we'll be uncomfortable and stressed. If we view it as enjoyable, it will help relieve stress.

Saki Santorelli, Associate Director of the Stress Reduction Clinic at the University of Massachusetts Medical Center, notes:

> *"How* one gardens is more important than *if* one gardens. It may be more important to invite people to pay careful attention to various aspects of gardening rather than to tell them to relax. A careful attention to spading, planting and weeding may cultivate an effortless, spontaneous 'relaxation' that arises from the very willingness to enter fully into the simple activity of gardening."

The focus is on paying attention to the current activity and becoming fully aware of it. Gardening provides a full range of mental, physical and sensory experiences. Compare any enjoyable activity that involves both mind and body to encounters common in the business world.

Imagine a business meeting where each manager has a different agenda and no one wants to give an inch. Someone questions your judgment. The adrenalin flows—with nowhere to go. You want to be somewhere else. You watch the clock. Your neck muscles tense. Your back stiffens. Your body is filled with tension, and there's no outlet for relief.

Many stressful situations are the result of not paying attention to what you're doing at the moment. When you misplaced your keys, you weren't paying attention to where you put them in the first place. When you miss an appointment or dent the fender of the car, you're probably daydreaming about some future or past event. Use gardening as a therapeutic tool to learn how to focus on the "here and now," and the task at hand.

Digging, chopping and hitting motions can help relieve stress and tension. Some experts advise purchasing a heavy bag and striking it. I advise striking the dirt with a hoe. Chop up corn stalks with a machete. Double dig garden beds with conviction. These strenuous activities can help relieve stress and provide an outlet for aggression. (For a more involved discussion on coping with anger and "self-talk", I highly recommend *When Anger Hurts, Quieting the Storm Within*, New Harbinger Publications 1989.)

If you need to relax and unwind, take a walk around the garden, stretch thoroughly both before and after your gardening workout, and enjoy the colors, textures and fragrances of the garden.

How to relax in the garden:

❀ Use markers in the garden. Every time you see one, stop, consciously relax, and breathe deeply in and out.

❀ Breathe, stretch and relax during your rest periods.

❀ After a period of exercise, stop and do nothing. Feel your breathing and repeat the word "relax."

❀ Attack digging beds, turning the compost and cultivating with the same vigor as weight lifting, wind sprints or swimming.

❀ Always reassess your fitness and gardening goals and objectives (Chapter 22).

❀ Follow the exercise cycle of stretching, warm-up, exercise and cool down while gardening.

❀ Listen to music while gardening.

❀ Teach a child how to garden. Remember, you're there for him.

❀ Repeat positive affirmations as you garden (Chapter 21).

❀ Make a short list of activities and stick to it. Don't try to do everything in one afternoon.

❀ Stop periodically and take a moment to see, hear, smell, touch and taste all that is around you. Smell the flowers, touch the leaves, listen to the birds and taste the vegetables.

❀ Volunteer to help with a horticultural therapy program. Working with individuals with physical, developmental or emotional disabilities will give you an appreciation for others and how horticulture can enrich lives.

Summary
Stress is a serious problem in our highly structured, fast-paced, modern lifestyle. Allow the natural rhythms of the garden to both slow you down and calm you. Pay attention to the garden experience, and you'll find yourself involved, absorbed and fulfilled.

Chapter Twenty

Horticultural Therapy

Horticultural therapy uses plants and horticultural activities to improve the social, educational, psychological, and physical well-being of people with disabilities.

Horticultural therapy involves structured and purposeful programs of goal-orientated activities tailored to the needs of a wide variety of individuals: those who are physically disabled, senior citizens, and substance abusers. As an adjunctive therapy it is unique because the medium is living.

The first known greenhouse for use by the mentally ill was built in Pennsylvania in 1879. After World War II, the federal government helped foster horticultural therapy through the widespread establishment of programs in veterans hospitals. Volunteers from garden clubs brought the physical and psychological benefits of gardening to thousands of patients from the war.

In 1955, Michigan State University awarded the first graduate degree in horticultural therapy. The first horticultural therapy undergraduate curriculum was established at Kansas State University in 1971.

The American Horticultural Therapy Association (AHTA), is a membership association founded in 1973 dedicated to promoting horticultural therapy and rehabilitation programs. The AHTA serves as a clearing house for ideas and as an advocate for programs that serve and train disabled individuals. The AHTA provides a forum for those involved in horticultural therapy to share ideas, a newsletter and a variety of publications. *The Journal of Therapeutic Horticulture* is included with a membership in the AHTA.

For people who are elderly or physically disabled, gardening offers a wide choice of activities that provide an outlet for creativity and a feeling of productiveness—from hoeing, planting and raking, to arranging flowers and shelling peas.

In the context of this book, horticultural therapy has a dual purpose. One, it helps redefine our perspective of fitness. Fitness now includes adults in wheelchairs, physically active and caring for plants; senior citizens gardening together, alert and active; and children with learning disabilities watering a flower or planting a seed. Second, the principles of horticultural therapy can be transferred to everyday people wanting to live a healthier, more fulfilling life but who have not found a consistent, long-term means to achieve their goal.

Horticultural Therapy Programs

Programs for People who are Physically Disabled or Elderly:

Success of a horticultural program may be attributed in part to the diversity of activities that make the program interesting to a wide group of people. Activities are tailored to the physical and mental capabilities of the individual. Potting plants, working at waist-high planters and using long-handled tools help provide meaningful activity to those with limited mobility.

Administrators of a horticultural therapy program should provide a climate that will:

- ❀ improve morale of the target population.
- ❀ encourage social interaction.
- ❀ promote cooperation between group members.
- ❀ increase self-confidence.
- ❀ enhance physical functioning.
- ❀ improve cognitive functioning (following steps).

A horticultural therapy program sponsored by Clemson University in a residential care facility was designed to meet the needs of the elderly. They grew vegetables, fruits and flowers. The goals of the program were to provide:

❀ an outlet for self-expression.
❀ variety from their institutionalized surroundings.
❀ a sense of personal control and independence.
❀ an environment conducive to social interaction.
❀ support and a feeling of service to others.
❀ mental, visual and auditory stimulation.
❀ exercise.

Nancy C. Stevenson, HTR, president of the American Horticultural Therapy Association (AHTA) adds:

"A year-round curriculum is best for those in a nursing-home environment. I've worked with programs that incorporate both indoor and outdoor gardening. A moveable cart with fluorescent bulbs or a greenhouse is used to start plants indoors. Clients are involved with all phases of horticulture: planting seeds, transplanting, maintaining plants through the summer, harvesting, and collecting everlastings and herbs for winter crafts. Clients work through the cycle of nature.

"The mild exercise provided by gardening is particularly useful for senior citizens. It uses their fingers and hands and keeps joints flexible.

"It is important that people have a psychological investment in something they have *mastery* over. In nursing homes, the residents may feel a sense of loss of control. Gardening gives a sense of mastery back to them and provides them with the opportunity to make positive changes in their environment.

"Gardening helps to reduce clients' self-absorption and gets them interested in tomorrow—not what happened yesterday. The elderly tend to dwell on the past—unfinished business in their lives. Gardening gives them something to anticipate and a renewed optimism about the future. Also, the social aspects of gardening are important. It's a group activity with common goals.

"It's not the activity, not the end product that's important. It's a *process* and a *tool* to develop relationships between patient and therapist. Groups really lighten up after the [horticulture] sessions. The textures and fragrances of cut flowers and dried herbs bring back favorable memories from their childhood."

As each generation ages, the benefits, physically, nutritionally, and emotionally of gardening become increasingly relevant. Gardening is a lifestyle that can be learned at any age and adapted as physical requirements change.

The *Gardening from the Heart* program for disadvantaged youth, adults and residential seniors is sponsored by the Men's Garden Clubs of America. It is currently active in thirty-two cities across the United States. The program partners with forty-three institutions using 250 gardening advisors (mostly retirees). The program benefits people who are:

- 🌸 disadvantaged.
- 🌸 mentally retarded.
- 🌸 physically handicapped.
- 🌸 emotionally disturbed.
- 🌸 in Veterans homes or hospitals.

The program's mission is "To extend the dividends of horticulture therapy to youth and adults, including the elderly, who are disadvantaged (emotionally disturbed, handicapped or retarded) by clubs establishing partnerships with institutions related."

Lloyd Kraft, National Chairman of Gardening from the Heart, adds: "Gardening has dividends as a therapy. For those who garden, raising plants provides satisfaction and pride of accomplishment." The program establishes a one on one relationship with the volunteer gardeners and institutionalized youths. The effect is a "father-son" mentoring relationship. He stresses that gardening activities are "supportive to therapeutic readjustment."

Physical Disabilities

A high school senior from Harrodsburg, Kentucky, suffered massive head injuries in a car accident. Horticultural therapy helped him during his recovery. He devised a garden with wheelchair aisles between the rows of corn, tomatoes, and bush beans. He developed special equipment to dig weeds, plant seeds and fertilize the crops. The techniques he used and the tools he developed were shared with other residents of the rehabilitation unit. In the first year, thirty-seven patients participated in the project.

The *Rehabilitation Center for the Blind* in Daytona Beach, Florida, provides horticultural therapy to legally blind adults. Harold Cardwell, HTR, is the director of the horticultural therapy program. It has two primary components:

> *Teaching "blind skills"*—the students learn how to "see" with their hands and fingers. Sensory training includes learning to identify plants by the shape, texture and smell of their leaves, stems and blossoms. For example, some plants have square stems, others round. Mr. Cardwell has observed that the students' sensory abilities appear to be enhanced more than others not in the horticultural therapy program.

> *Teaching vocational skills*—students work in the greenhouse and on the grounds. They learn skills for potential employment in theme, county and state parks. The program duration is six months. Mr Cardwell says, "Our placement is over fifty percent, whereas the national average is only twenty-five."

Mr. Cardwell had many inspiring stories from his personal experience:

> "Plants have a certain attraction, even if you're blind and deaf. It doesn't matter. Students learn to use their senses of smell and touch.

> "One lady in our program was blind, had arthritis and couldn't bend over. Yet gardening was her life. We cut

fourteen, 55 gallon drums lengthwise, and set them up waist level in the garden. She grew vegetables and flowers. Her garden was the most beautiful I've ever seen.

"A blind girl learned how to grow and raise plants in the greenhouse. She told me that it was the first time something *depended on her*. That small yet profound experience turned her life around.

"For those with congenital blindness (blind all their life) there is a magic moment when they plant a tomato seed, and in a few days return to find a growing, living seedling. They're hooked and ready for the next activity.

"It's a shame, that in tough economic times, the horticultural therapy program is the first to go. Considering the benefits it provides, the opposite should be true. A blind person can't get out and jog or run as readily as a sighted person. A garden is convenient. Lifting plants and tools provides exercise. Knowing that the plants depend on you is fulfilling."

Horticultural therapy and neighborhood gardening programs are relatively inexpensive to start, yet provide so many benefits. Caring for plants provides a sense of personal satisfaction. Learning horticulture provides employment for individuals with disabilities. Gardening provides food to eat. Horticultural therapy benefits those most who have few other alternatives for exercise and meaningful activity.

The Enid A. Haupt Glass Garden at the *Howard A. Rusk Institute of Rehabilitative Medicine* in New York City provides horticultural therapy services to individuals with physical disabilities, including strokes, birth abnormalities and brain-damaged, head trauma.

A fully wheelchair accessible greenhouse provides a variety of activities that can be continued after the patients' discharge. Specific tasks are designed to help them improve eye/hand coordination and spatial organization. For others, the focus is on building strength, endurance, cognitive skills and cooperative group activity.

Individuals with Learning Disabilities

Williston High School in Florida implemented a pilot gardening program for learning disabled children, ages 8-12. Simple gardening activities were taught to the children to help them:

❀ develop a positive view of order and structure.
❀ recognize the value of change.
❀ accept their roles as agents of change.
❀ discover growth as a developmental concept.
❀ learn the value of cooperative effort.
❀ cultivate positive relationships with adults.

The *Melwood Horticultural Training Center, Inc.*, in Upper Marlboro, Maryland, is a diversified organization assisting adult persons with developmental disabilities (primarily with mental retardation) with vocational training and employment services. Melwood's goals are to assist persons with developmental disabilities to become productive, contributing members of society through becoming self-empowered, economically independent and by having choices of friends, work, and play.

The greenhouse production of plants and the landscaping and grounds maintenance services develop within developmentally-disabled persons a sense of discipline, manual dexterity, and work skills. Melwood incorporates behavior modification techniques in the form of wages, rewards (bonuses, instructor approval, peer recognition) and job responsibility. The horticultural environment has proven to be excellent in fostering human development through the use of behavior modification, task analysis, modeling and on-the-job training. In addition, the center sells what the trainees create providing them with a sense of satisfaction.

A horticultural therapy program at the *Florida Alcoholism Treatment Center* addresses major issues in substance-abuse treatment:

> ❀ raising self-esteem.
> ❀ helping the patient act in a more responsible manner.
> ❀ establishing leisure-time skills that can fill the void left by not using drugs and alcohol.

The patients in the horticultural program at the Alcoholic Treatment Center:

> ❀ learned how to start plants in a greenhouse.
> ❀ learned to start cuttings in a mist propagation bed.
> ❀ were introduced to the benefits of the use of compost in gardening by establishing a compost pile.
> ❀ were provided experience with a specific group of plants through a community rose garden.
> ❀ were introduced to the joy of growing something useful and beneficial through a community vegetable garden.

Bibby Moore, HTR, author of *Growing with Gardening*, has master degrees in clinical social work and environmental management—in essence how to improve the human condition through the environment. In her work with prison populations she noticed how gardening gives them a sense of self-esteem. Ms. Moore adds:

> "Horticultural therapy is a motivational tool to get people out of depression and low self-esteem. It gives them a sense of success. Plants are non-judgmental.

> "Growing plants provides a sense of control: the inmates feel they have control, can impose order in their life—yet it [gardening] always offers something new and unknown.

> "One of the reasons I wrote *Growing with Gardening* was to get doctors to understand the significance of gardening and write a prescription."

That last insight I find particularly interesting: It's the same reason I wrote *Fitness the Dynamic Gardening Way.*

I highly recommend Ms. Moore's book:

Growing with Gardening—A Twelve-Month Guide for Therapy, Recreation and Education by Bibby Moore (The University of North Carolina Press, 1988, P.O. Box 2288, Dept. FG, Chapel Hill, NC, 27515-2288 $14.95 paper; $29.95 cloth).

It's packed with useful activities for a successful horticultural therapy program.

Diane Relf, H.T.M., Ph.D., an Extension Specialist with the Department of Horticulture at Virginia Tech, has identified seven benefits of the plant/people interaction:

1) *Integration of Biological and Psychological Factors*—Often, recently disabled persons have difficulty relating their disability to their sense of worth. Horticulture helps them create something useful that "also needs care."
2) *Mastery of the Environment*—Those in nursing homes, hospitals and the inner-city, have a sense of lost control. Interacting with plants shows them that their actions can change their surroundings.
3) *Work Substitute*—Horticulture provides activity for senior citizens and disabled persons who are not able to work in traditional occupations.
4) *Responsibility*—Research has shown that giving elderly residents in a nursing home responsibility over care of plants improved their alertness, active participation and general sense of well-being.
5) *Creativity*—Horticulture offers many outlets for expression.
6) *Frustration Tolerance*—Things go wrong and plants die. Learning to cope with death and small frustrations helps patients learn to deal with everyday life.
7) *Intense Concentration*—Research by Rachael Kaplan, Ph.D., a psychologist at the University of Michigan, has shown that gardening sustains "involuntary attention." This attention is what helps patients forget worries and cares.

In an interview with Dr. Relf, she said, "A well-cared-for plant entered in a local flower show will have an equal chance of winning regardless of any impairment its grower may have. Plants are a great equalizer among people."

Dr. Relf is coordinator of the People-Plant Council (PPC). Its mission it "to document and communicate the effect that plants and flowers have on human well-being and improved life-quality." The council's five part strategy focuses on the effects that plants have on human well-being through the psychological, sociological, physiological, economic and environmental effects they produce. Affiliation is open to all organizations within the horticulture and social science community. If you're interested in joining the PPC, Dr. Relf's address is listed on page 271 in the Appendix.

A constant theme throughout horticultural therapy research is that horticulture, working with plants, *demands action*. You get your hands dirty. You plant a seed. The plants respond to your care. Activities can be as simple as putting seeds between damp paper towels, or as complicated as doing landscape architecture. Results are both short-term—growing radishes or marigolds, and long-term—harvesting fruits and nuts from trees planted several years ago.

Vegetable Gardens for Those with Special Physical Requirements
Individuals with limited walking movement should use narrow, two or three foot wide garden beds, raised twenty-four to thirty-six inches. Paths should be three to four feet wide and set with bricks or other hard material that will allow a wheelchair to maneuver in the garden. This will allow physically restricted individuals to be able to weed and cultivate without having to stretch or bend over.

Equip garden tools with extra long handles, giving those with limited mobility access to all areas. Specialty weeders are available to grab or snip a weed at soil level. Set up large earthen pots or waist-high garden boxes on a patio or deck. Tillers and cultivators greatly reduce physical demands for preparing and weeding garden beds. Establish garden beds close to the house.

Tools can be adapted to an individual's needs. Velcro strips can be added to handles to improve grip. Hoes or rakes with short handles can be used in raised, waist-high beds by those in a sitting position. Use scissors with a spring action for cutting stems. The Easy Kneeler, available from Gardeners Supply, has a sturdy frame that allows a person to raise and lower her body with her arms and a pad for kneeling. Two-wheeled garden carts are easier to push and balance than the traditional wheelbarrow.

Summary

The versatility of horticultural therapy is best illustrated by the target populations it serves. Over the years it has helped people with:

* learning disabilities.
* mental disabilities.
* physical disabilities.
* developmental disabilities.
* emotional disabilities.
* substance addiction.
* visual impairment.

In addition, geriatric patients, inmates in correctional institutions and the homeless have benefitted from horticultural therapy.

It is no longer *just* gardening. Growing fruits, vegetables and flowers has been proven to be a valuable, powerful psychological therapy. Nurturing and growing plants has been part of our civilization for thousands of years. Our fascination and interest in growing things is more than just plants, dirt and clay pots. Growing plants increases our awareness of the environment and our relationship to it. While the world around us changes dramatically and technological wonders continue to amuse and bemuse us, the relationship between men/women, plants and the earth remains constant.

In a sense, the garden is a metaphor for life. As Ms. Moore notes: "Gardening helps us develop a relationship with the environment and its cycles of growth and change." The lessons of life—success, failure, patience, life and death—are all experienced many times each season in the garden. Use the garden to learn how to enjoy the moment, change what you can and accept what you cannot. These valuable lessons are, so often, learned too late in life.

In only the last five years, the field of horticultural therapy has expanded greatly. Research is in place to refine this process and expand its ability to help disadvantaged individuals lead productive, healthy, happy lives. The theory and procedures behind horticultural therapy are similar to *Fitness the Dynamic Gardening Way*. Horticulture can be used by *anyone* to lead a better, more fulfilling life. As a health and wellness lifestyle, it provides:

❀ a therapy that is flexible and adaptable to individual needs.
❀ aerobic and muscle-toning exercise.
❀ fresh, nutritious fruits and vegetables.
❀ a variety of interesting activities.
❀ stimulation for your senses.
❀ feedback as plants respond to your care.
❀ a feeling of accomplishment.
❀ an aesthetic, creative outlet for expression.
❀ a sense of being part of the environment.

Chapter Twenty-One

Visualization

Creative visualization is a psychological technique by which you imagine you have already accomplished a future goal. You see, feel, touch, taste and smell everything and everyone in this new environment.

A wealth of excellent books is available on this subject: *Unlimited Power*, *Psychocybernetics*, *Creative Visualization*, *You Will See it When You Believe It* and *Imagineering*. I highly recommend them.

Hope Weisel, M.S., R.D., of St. Luke's Roosevelt Hospital Center for Weight Control in New York City, states that "Visualization techniques play a big part in working with obese patients. We ask them to imagine themselves at a wedding, what they wear and what they eat. Visualization techniques help them feel more comfortable in a familiar setting as a different, slimmer person."

Gardening your way to a slimmer, healthier, happier you is ideally suited to visualization techniques. The gardening experience is so rich in colors, sights, smells, tastes, and tactile stimulation, that it will be both easy and very enjoyable to imagine yourself, the way you wish yourself to be, in your beautiful, lush, Garden of Eden.

To accomplish this, first write down all the characteristics of the *ideal you* in the *ideal garden*. Use big sheets of paper and lots of color. Buy a box of sixty-four Crayola crayons. Find some books or magazines on gardening and use them as guides for your perfect garden. Use fashion or bodybuilding magazines for your ideal body. Spare no expense. Let your imagination wander. Have fun.

Close your eyes, and picture the ideal you in the ideal garden exercising, planting, and harvesting fresh fruits and vegetables. Every action that moves you closer to the ideal garden will subconsciously and automatically move you closer to the ideal, fit and healthy you.

Write down on your piece of paper all the characteristics of this "imagined you." Draw a picture. How do your friends treat you? What do your parents say and do? What do your children say and do? How does it feel to go out? Walk around your garden and admire yourself. Feel the sun and a cool breeze on your face and body as you walk around your ideal garden. It is important to visualize the ideal you and your ideal garden as if they have already happened.

In your mind, start the plants from seed. Watch them germinate. Harden them off in a cold-frame. Plant them in the garden. Watch them thrive, tall and strong.

Imagine the garden, the sun glistening off dew drops on snow peas high on a trellis. Reach for one. Pick it. Put it into your mouth and chew. Feel it crunch in your mouth and burst forth with natural goodness. The garden is filled with an array of beautiful, vibrant colors: white, pink, red, blue, orange, yellow. All the plants and flowers you love: roses, lilies, hollyhocks, petunias—whatever you want. They're all there at the peak of bloom.

Look at grass clippings, leaves and kitchen scraps not as waste for the landfill but as the "stuff of life" as they slowly transform into compost. Visualize the garden and all the flowers, fruits and vegetables bursting out of the compost pile.

Everyone remarks about your "green thumb." Neighbors stop by and smile at the blooming flowers. They gaze in awe at your tomato plants, growing out and over six-foot wire cages. Visualize a basket full of red tomatoes, green peppers, eggplant, basil, oregano, and green beans. Feel it, touch it, taste it, smell it. Hear the birds sing and the crickets chirp.

From *your* hands, all this is done. Think of the ideal garden and the attractive, toned, ideal you in the past tense. It has already happened. Experience this in your mind.

After you have attained your ideal weight and state of fitness, what will you do next? Imagine this new situation. Do you add more garden beds? Do you attempt to grow more difficult plants? Maybe you join a dance class. Perhaps you decide to share your love of gardening with disadvantaged children or senior citizens. Maybe you start jogging, swimming or cycling and gardening becomes your cross-training exercise. Treat yourself to a night on the town. In your mind, go out to your favorite restaurant. Enjoy yourself. You're a good person. Gardening is good for you. You've earned the right to be happy.

Make an audio tape with a text similar to the previous example. The first part should relax your body. The tape should start like this:

"Make yourself comfortable, either sitting in a chair or lying down with your arms at your side. Take a deep, slow breath. Breathe in, and gently exhale. Feel your toes, let them relax. Breathe in deeply and gently exhale. Feel your legs, let them relax. Breathe in deeply, and as you exhale, allow all the stress and worry of the day to flow right out of your body. Feel your stomach. Let it relax. Every time you breathe out, feel your body relaxing, sinking deeper and deeper. Feel your arms. Let them relax. Repeat the word 'relax.' Every time you repeat the word 'relax' feel your body loosening, sinking, freeing itself from the stress and anxiety of the day. Feel your abdomen. Let it relax. Breathe in, and slowly exhale. Feel your chest as you breathe, and breathe slowly and evenly, as if you were asleep . . . ."

Continue as above to relax your arms, neck, back, and face. Always breathe deeply and slowly. Complete relaxation texts can be found in *Guide to Stress Reduction* by L. John Mason, Ph. D.

(Peace Press 1980), and *Self Esteem* by Matthew McKay, Ph.D., and Patrick Fanning (New Harbinger Publications 1987). These two books cover stress, self-talk and visualization in greater detail.

After you're relaxed, add your personal ideal garden and ideal you portion. You will be transported to this magical, future you and come to believe it to be real, as if it had already happened. Modify the content to suit your unique goals.

Listen to your tape every day. Make a list of positive affirmations and repeat them several times each day. Write them down on index cards and paste them to the mirror in your bathroom, to the dashboard of your car and the door of the refrigerator. At first, repeating your positive affirmations may be uncomfortable. That is perfectly normal. If you've been told you're a certain way your entire life and now believe it as fact, changing your internal image of yourself will produce discomfort.

It may take weeks and even months for your image of yourself to change. Eventually, you will be *more* comfortable with the *new, visualized you* than the old you. This is good. Your thoughts will motivate you to change your behavior and *act* like the ideal you.

The reason many never garden, never lose weight, and never are truly happy is that they're not comfortable with *that* positive image of themselves. They continue with negative self-talk such as "I don't have a 'green thumb.' I've tried diets with doctors before and they never worked. I've spent thousands on exercise equipment and failed." They replay these irrational, negative thoughts, over and over.

When I first gardened, it felt awkward to grow food for my family. I wasn't a gardener. I didn't have a green thumb. I'd never grown vegetables before, but I was so drawn to the *process* of gardening that I never let my failures interfere with my vision of a perfect garden, a perfect harvest and a perfect dinner with my family.

I'll never forget first reading about composting. Here was a process that had been around since the dawn of nature, and I had never been aware of it. The next day, I borrowed a friend's truck and visited a horse stable nearby that had mounds of aged manure free to anyone who wanted it. I created a circular compost bin out of old chicken wire and filled it to the top. The next day I could feel heat from the pile as the aged manure decomposed and transformed into compost. I was ecstatic.

When you first adopt gardening as a comprehensive exercise and diet regimen, you must "suspend reality" and have faith that your dreams will be realized. Setbacks are temporary. You must believe that the ideal garden and the ideal you are real—today. It has already happened and it feels good. And you're *comfortable* feeling good. (This may sound trite, but it's amazing how many people prefer to be miserable. They feel that if all goes well, some disaster is about to befall them.)

Soon, almost by magic, instead of procrastinating on the couch, you're outside preparing the garden beds. Instead of making excuses, you're starting plants under fluorescent lights. Instead of sleeping in on Saturday and feeling listless and bored, you jump out of bed, throw on your clothes and race to the back yard to exercise in the garden.

As the fat slowly disappears, your muscles strengthen, you increase flexibility and endurance and you eat the best-tasting produce available, you'll learn that, for once, the reality is as good as the dream. You'll feel better about yourself, both inside and out.

Summary
You've embarked on a lifelong health and wellness program. Take a few moments and work on the visualization exercises. It's *your* responsibility to make sure you're thinking positive thoughts and moving toward your goals in life. No one can do this for you. Use gardening as a tool to build self-esteem and self-awareness. Combine your gardening and fitness goals into one. Visualization is a powerful psychological technique. Believe in this, and wonderful things will happen to your life. The day I believed in the power of visualization is the day I started to write this book. *And it happened.*

Positive Affirmations

The statements below replace "negative self-talk" we often repeat to ourselves throughout the day. Use the ones you like, and feel free to add your own. Write them down on a card, and repeat them several times each day.

- ❀ I'm a good gardener.
- ❀ I'm a good person because I'm aware of the garden and enjoy the beauty and wonders of nature.
- ❀ The birds and beneficial insects in the garden are my friends.
- ❀ Every season, I'm a better gardener.
- ❀ Gardening relaxes me.
- ❀ Turning the compost strengthens me.
- ❀ Weeding and hoeing strengthens my legs.
- ❀ The soil smells good.
- ❀ I enjoy the feel of raking the soil in early spring.
- ❀ I am helping reduce the amount of waste in the landfill by composting table scraps, grass clippings and leaves.
- ❀ It's great to be alive.
- ❀ I am grateful for this day and being able to exercise in my garden and grow fresh fruits and vegetables.
- ❀ My garden is beautiful.
- ❀ My family and friends enjoy the vegetables I grow.
- ❀ The vegetables I grow are worthy of a five-star restaurant.
- ❀ I cooperate *with* nature to grow vegetables organically.
- ❀ I love my garden.
- ❀ The worries of the world are behind me while I'm in the garden.
- ❀ I'm a good person because I care about the environment.
- ❀ This moment is precious. I feel, see, smell, taste and touch all that is around me.
- ❀ Whenever I can, I share the joy of gardening with a neighbor or friend.
- ❀ Gardening helps me be a better athlete.

Chapter Twenty-Two

Gardening by Objectives

We've examined the exercise, nutritional, and psychological benefits of gardening. To tie everything together, we'll borrow a technique from business management. Setting goals and strategies is common in the business world. *GOSPA* stands for:

Goals
Objectives
Strategies
Plans
Activities

GOSPA principles will help you carry out a successful health and wellness program the Dynamic Gardening Way.

A *goal* is a *general description* of what you want to accomplish. Often called a mission statement, it sums up what you want to achieve in one or two sentences.

Objectives differ from goals because they always have a *measurable target* and *specific achievement date*. Measurements can be pushups completed, bushels of vegetables grown or pounds lost. The time-frame can be today, this week or a year from now.

Quantifying your objectives within a time-frame provides *feedback*. Did you achieve your objectives? Was your strategy effective? If it wasn't, what prevented you from achieving your objectives? The feedback process is essential to learning from your mistakes and correcting your course of action.

Strategies are *how* you achieve your goals and objectives. Whether it's gardening, exercise, chess or war, there are always many options *how* you reach your goal.

One gardening strategy would be to design a free-form wildflower garden of native wildflowers and shade-loving ornamentals. A contrasting strategy would be a formal English, knot-herb garden.

You may decide to be a world-class athlete. One strategy would be to win at all costs. This could include the use of steroids, a dangerous and illegal drug. The other strategy would be building strength and muscle mass by working out harder and eating nutritious food.

Plans are a series of *activities* you intend to accomplish in the near future. A plan may include several activities, which are the *actions* prescribed by your strategy and plans to reach your objectives.

Another important concept is the difference between *effectiveness* and *efficiency*. Effectiveness is how well you achieved your objectives. You may have been on a hundred diets and know everything about dieting and exercise, but if you're still not pleased with your weight, your diet and exercise program has not been effective.

Efficiency is *how well* you use your *time* and *resources*. You can do a task efficiently—maximizing resources—but still not achieve your objectives. You may spend hours planting vegetables. They may be organized neatly in rows. You use the best tools—but your harvests are poor. You're an efficient gardener but not a very effective one. You may be efficient in planning meals with carefully thought-out lists. You eat very little but still can't lose weight because you cannot find an exercise program that fits your schedule. Your diet program may be efficient, but it's not effective as a weight-loss program.

Therefore, you can be efficient but not effective. Likewise, you might not be particularly efficient but always get good results. A good example of this would be the salesperson who is always rushed, can never find his reports, is never on time, and a constant irritation to all—yet always exceeds quota.

The concepts of efficiency and effectiveness play an important role in the GOSPA model. The greatest error occurs when you invest an inordinate amount of time in making a task efficient but it's not effective. This leads to feelings of failure and frustration. The next few pages list examples of gardening *and* fitness Goals, Objectives, Strategies and Activities. Plans are groups of activities in sequence. Use them to develop your own personal fitness and dynamic gardening goals.

Goals

❀ Establish gardening as a primary vehicle for diet and exercise.

❀ Add dynamic gardening as a cross-training complement to your exercise regimen.

❀ Grow and use medicinal and therapeutic plants and herbs.

❀ Garden to spend more time with your family.

❀ Live to be 100.

❀ Live a healthy and productive life.

❀ Provide pesticide-free fruits and vegetables for your family.

❀ Transform your lifestyle from a destructive one to a healthy one.

❀ Use gardening to help stop smoking (substitute one activity for another).

❀ Adopt "green," environmentally conscious principles (recycling, composting, conserving water).

❀ Grow expensive vegetables to save money on grocery bills.

❀ Grow large quantities of vegetables to can, dry and freeze for winter.

❀ Establish a community garden to benefit the neighborhood.

❀ Establish a youth gardening program at your church.

❀ Work with a senior citizens horticultural therapy project.

❀ Establish a barrier-free garden for individuals with physical disabilities.

Objectives

❀ Double dig one 3' x 12' bed this spring.

❀ Visit four local nurseries this spring, and choose one as your local supplier.

❀ Grow tomatoes, peppers, eggplant, zucchini and basil this summer.

❀ Lose twenty pounds within six months.

❀ Substitute dynamic gardening one or two days a week for traditional aerobics.

❀ Establish six raised beds this calendar year.

❀ Be able to do three sets of six chinups by the end of summer.

❀ Save $500 on grocery bills this year.

❀ Establish a successful seed-starting system in the next six weeks.

❀ Start 200 perennial plants from seed this season.

❀ Plant a spring, summer and fall garden this year, even if it's only three or four different vegetables.

❀ Grow the earliest tomatoes on the block this spring.

❀ Substitute fresh herbs from the garden for salt at least one meal each week.

❀ Raise money to donate seeds, seed-starting supplies and gardening tools to a senior citizens home or youth group this spring.

❀ Take a horticultural therapy class at your local educational facility or through the mail this year.

❀ Work with your hands for ten minutes each day arranging flowers, repotting plants or drying herbs.

Strategies

❀ Transfer exercise time to gardening time.

❀ Grow all plants from seed.

❀ Grow only heirloom vegetable varieties (no hybrids).

❀ Grow only disease-resistant hybrids.

❀ Buy all plants from local nurseries.

❀ Use only organic fertilizers and pesticides.

❀ Use Integrated Pest Management (IPM) to control insect pests (use chemicals as a last resort).

❀ Use whatever means possible to extend early spring and late fall gardening seasons.

❀ Adopt organic gardening techniques but not intensive gardening techniques (deep-dug beds).

❀ Always garden with a friend or family member.

❀ Don't use any fungicide-treated seed.

❀ Save seed from existing heirloom vegetable plants whenever possible.

❀ Use a lawn or garden service as a backup when time doesn't permit proper garden maintenance.

❀ Keep a perfectly neat and weed-free garden.

❀ Grow a formal herb garden. Emphasis is on neatness and appearance.

❀ Grow an informal wildflower garden. Emphasize free-form design with native plants that tolerate neglect.

❀ Minimize grass mowing area with wildflower plantings, heavy mulch and ground covers.

❀ Start a small garden, and use local organic farmers for the bulk of your fresh fruits and vegetables.

Activities

❀ Go to a gardening show.

❀ Join a gardening club.

❀ Plant a specific herb, fruit or vegetable (Sage, basil, asparagus, blueberries)

❀ Start a gardening diary.

❀ Take pictures of your garden.

❀ Build a Circuit Training structure (dip bar, grape arbor,sit-up board).

❀ Build a raised bed.

❀ Buy a tiller.

❀ Install a drip-irrigation system.

❀ Throw out all the diet pills and powders in your cabinets.

❀ Throw out all your chemical pesticides.

❀ Walk around the neighborhood, and find a gardening buddy.

❀ Test your soil.

❀ Record an audio tape of your ideal garden and ideal you, using visualization techniques.

❀ Buy a chipper/shredder.

❀ Build a compost bin.

❀ Go to the library, and check out three books on gardening.

❀ Subscribe to a national gardening magazine.

❀ Watch a television gardening show each week.

❀ Join a gardening association.

❀ Prepare a 4' x 8' raised vegetable bed.

❀ Plant an apple tree.

❀ Adapt existing tools for individuals with limited hand or arm movement.

❀ Construct a waist-high garden bed.

❀ Buy a book on visualization techniques and *use* it.

❀ Repeat positive affirmations every day.

❀ Spend twenty minutes in the garden walking and cultivating while paying attention to stretching your body.

The Dynamic Gardening Way Planning Guide

NAME:_____   DATE:_____

Goal

Objectives	
Health	
Wellness	
Weight Loss	
Physical Appearance	
Other Health Objectives	
Gardening	
Vegetables	
Fruit Trees & Berry Bushes	
Herbs	
Flowers	
Other Gardening Objectives	

The Dynamic Gardening Way Planning Guide

NAME:_____   DATE:_____

Strategies	
Health	
Wellness	
Weight Loss	
Physical Appearance	
Other Health Objectives	
Gardening	
Vegetables	
Fruit Trees & Berry Bushes	
Herbs	
Flowers	
Other Gardening Objectives	

The Dynamic Gardening Way Planning Guide

NAME:_____   DATE:_____

Activities	
Health	
Wellness	
Weight Loss	
Physical Appearance	
Other Health Goals	
Gardening	
Vegetables	
Fruit Trees & Berry Bushes	
Herbs	
Flowers	
Other Objectives	

Chapter Twenty-Three

Gardening with Children

Note to aunts, uncles and grandparents . . . .

Although I refer to "my children" or "your children" often in this book, please note that they can *also* be your grandchildren, nieces or nephews. They could be the children at your church or youth group. I feel it's essential that we bring the pleasures and benefits of gardening to our youth. Most have never experienced gardening. My hope is that the dynamic gardening approach will change their perceptions of gardening. The next two chapters provide examples on how to relate gardening to what children enjoy.

Children are tuned to the world around them. Present gardening as play and their imagination and creativity flourish. Children love learning and discovering things for themselves. They will return to the garden again and again when it's fun and interesting. Just remember that a child's attention span is short.

Children love to accomplish a task and prove they're "grownup." Small successes, so much a part of the gardening experience, have a big impact on a young child's self-esteem.

Always *ask* them to join you in the garden. Never order them. Allowing them to follow their instincts gives them the freedom to love and appreciate the garden.

Grow lights and the Accelerated Propagation System (APS)™.

The APS self-watering system, fluorescent shop lights, and an automatic timer provide a controlled environment where you can grow virtually any number of plants from seed with little effort. I worked for a company that donated the APS system to an elementary school sixth-grade class. The students called it the "Green Thumb Machine." I'll always remember the children's smiles as they pulled me by the hand to see their plants growing in the trays. They felt successful, like they had accomplished something important. *And they had.*

Children are very responsive to the positive reinforcement from watching their plants grow. Besides the usual marigolds, with the APS they can grow more challenging and interesting plants, such as blackberry lilies, butterfly weed, coreopsis, dianthus, and stokesia.

Children's Garden Beds

Establish a garden bed specifically for children. Teach them how to hold tools properly. Help them prepare the soil and plant their seeds. Radishes and beans are particularly quick-growing. Tomatoes, peppers, peas, marigolds and zinnias are easy to grow. Grow fruits and vegetables they like: tomatoes, strawberries, blueberries, watermelons, honeydews, and cantaloupes.

Use a Positive Reinforcement System (stickers, stars, cold cash)

The value of some gardening activities may not be immediately apparent to small children. Therefore, the more mundane activities can carry rewards like stickers or tokens. Reward their gardening activity along with making the bed, brushing their teeth, doing their homework and going to bed on time. My wife and I tried this approach with our young children. They never failed to remind us how many stars they earned each night.

Each week they can redeem points for a toy, gift or money. Children respond very well to this positive, shaping approach. Over time, they will associate gardening with the things they love—which is about the best a gardening parent can hope for. As the years pass, they will understand *why* the beds are dug deeply, *why* compost is created, and *why* weeding is important.

Learn About Nature

Create a garden to attract butterflies, beneficial insects, toads, frogs and birds. Shasta daisies, hollyhocks, ageratum, French marigolds, zinnia, tithonia, butterfly weed and parsley all attract butterflies.

Cooperating *with* nature instills an appreciation of its wonders. The back yard becomes a science exhibit and a wildlife habitat. In the balance of nature, beneficial insects, spiders, earthworms, birds, and toads all have a role in improving the soil or eating insect pests.

Using a scavenger hunt approach, my six-year-old boy hunted for earthworms as I turned the compost pile. Later that week, we went fishing and used the worms for bait. We ate the fish with fresh new potatoes and tomatoes from the garden. Worms, fish, potatoes and tomatoes—all interconnected and part of a delightful afternoon with my son.

One day, we searched the broccoli plants for cabbage worms. My boy's eyes grew wide as he watched a parasitic wasp alight on a plant, bite a caterpillar in half, grab one end, and fly off. This might seem cruel, but it was an important lesson that no book, no television show, and no teacher could have taught better.

One afternoon, my three-year-old daughter dug a hole for new tomato plants and found two white grubs in the dirt. She called them "worms" and asked me what they were doing there. I told her they lived in the dirt and would grow up to be beetles someday. My boy named one "Squirmy." They played with the two grubs for a few minutes, and he asked, "Can I squash them with my shovel?" I told him it was his choice: put them back in the dirt where they would live or squash and kill them. He thought for just a second and put them back in the dirt. I was proud of him. At the age of six, he had already gained an appreciation for life, even that of a lowly grub.

Identify Plants

Ask children to identify the plants and vegetables they grow. Draw up flash cards with pictures of the vegetable, plant and seed on the front, and relevant growing information on the back. Work with them each year until they can identify a plant during all stages in its life cycle. Another interesting challenge is matching the seeds with the plants they grow.

Harvest Vegetables with the Children

Always include the children when harvesting vegetables. I'll always remember picking strawberries with my children. They greeted me every day for several weeks to pick the red, ripe strawberries—most were eaten before we entered the house.

Pick Flowers for Dinner Table or School

Every day, the children can pick flowers for the dinner table or take them to school. They can use dried flowers for flower arrangements and crafts.

Exercise with Child-Size Hoes, Rakes and Shovels

Encourage children to follow the exercise principles outlined in this book using three-quarter-size shovels, rakes and hoes. Teach them to use repetitions and sets and use their legs while digging and planting. They'll learn how the effort expended in the garden provides fresh food while keeping them fit. (Tools available from Smith and Hawken.)

As they grow older, they'll enjoy the garden as part of a healthy lifestyle. They can use the Circuit Training program to prepare for team sports such as football, baseball and soccer. Exercising while gardening can be both an alternative and *complement* to competitive team sports.

The Video Arcade Approach to Gardening

Video arcade games, particularly the home variety, have swept up our nation's youth. They play these games for hours, days and (gulp!) weeks. Why are children drawn to these electronic marvels? They're colorful, fast-paced, mysterious and cleverly designed to challenge and amuse children just enough to hold their attention.

Most games have a similar arrangement. You earn points by defeating armies of bad guys. After you defeat them you complete a "level" and move to the next one. Many games have eight levels of play, each more difficult than the previous one.

Throughout a game, there are typically all kinds of surprises, tricks, secret passages and any number of prized objects. Some offer bonus points; some allow you to skip a level and others give special powers or a "super weapon."

You're probably asking, "What does this have to do with gardening?" With a little ingenuity, we can apply these same principles to gardening.

Small, Incremental Successes:

Video games are a behavioral scientist's dream. Behavioral psychology, popularized by the late B. F. Skinner, is based on the premise of positive reinforcement—if a behavior is followed by a reward, the probability increases you will repeat the behavior. After you beat the first bad guy, you want to beat the next; after you catch the first fish, you can't wait for the second; and after the first radish sprouts from the ground, you want to plant another.

Video games are cleverly designed to be difficult, but not *too* difficult. They offer just enough challenge to keep you playing for hours, days, weeks and months. Let's use the same behavioral principles while gardening.

Establish a point system with levels for activities in the garden. Plant easy-to-grow vegetables: snap beans, radishes and tomatoes. Each year, add more challenge to your child's gardening activity list. Grow pumpkins, and write your child's name on each one as it forms. Have them care for their "personal" pumpkins.

Get your child in the habit of helping you for short periods each day. Even if it is only five minutes to pull a weed or plant a corn seed. Finish this simple task and tell them, "Thank you for helping. That's all for now, you can go play." If they wish to stay, praise them and find a small task for them to master. If they want to play let them go. Stay with it. Always show them how much fun you're having.

Exciting Colors, Sounds:

Video games always have exciting graphics, color, animation and music. The garden does too. At every opportunity invite your children out to the garden to see the seedlings emerge from the soil; show them colorful flowers; listen to the birds, crickets, cicadas, and frogs; discover beneficial insects in the garden.

Surprises, Intrigue:

Your character in a video game can jump up in the middle of nowhere, a box appears, and out pops a mushroom that gives you another life. This is the world of the popular "Mario Brothers"™ video game series. Children are always trading secrets, hints and tips about hidden rewards and perils of their favorite video games.

Arrange the garden to offer the same kind of surprises and excitement. Arrange a convenient critter of choice—a praying mantis, toad or turtle—in a strategic place in the garden. Create a series of flash cards, and set them in certain locations in the garden. The children receive a prize when they collect all the cards.

If the garden has a wide variety of flowers, herbs, vegetables and bushes, surprises will happen naturally. Beautiful butterflies will visit the garden; an orb spider will build a stunning concentric circular web; or a beautiful cyan stokesia flower will bloom that day.

Win Points, Move up a Level:

Older video games were played for only points. The newer ones have levels of play. This is not by chance but emerged from careful analysis of what motivates children. Not only is the idea of moving up a level part of the video game popularity, it is a microcosm of life itself: pass first grade and go to second; break your boards and move from red belt to black belt; score a touchdown and move from second string to first string; win a big sales order and you're promoted.

Gardening also has levels. It has seasons, levels of complexity and levels of harvest. As the children learn the difference between the good bugs and bad bugs, they move up a level. As they learn the difference between flowers and weeds, they move up a level.

As they successfully grow one type of vegetable they move up to another, more difficult one.

Concentration:

Video games require concentration. Just try calling your son, daughter or grandchild for dinner when they're in the middle of a game. Learning to concentrate on a task is an important skill.

In the garden, keep the children focused on short, achievable tasks. Have them prepare and plant a small portion of a garden bed, and as soon as they're finished let them play with their friends. Have them count the number of daisies, ladybugs, or butterflies they can find in the garden. Reward them with points, gold stars or a movie.

Eye/Hand Coordination:

There is no question that video games develop eye/hand coordination. But it's a very *fine* eye/hand coordination. Raking, hoeing, and weeding the garden, especially using the techniques described in this book, develop a *general* degree of eye/hand coordination. Gardening uses large muscle groups. Teach your child to move smoothly, stand up straight, use his legs, and alternate his grip.

Mastery At a Young Age:

A child's world is full of frustration, awkwardness, parental authority and a continual search for self-esteem. You need only watch a young child play a video game to see what mastery of a task means to him. Each video game creates a new world with a new set of rules. For most adults these imaginary worlds are difficult to learn. Children, however, adapt well to novel situations and excel. I'll never forget my boy chanting, "and I'm better than dad."

Succeeding at growing plants at a very young age will improve your child's self-esteem, pride and a yearning for more. A seed planted by a small child will grow the same as one planted by a Master Gardener. The plant doesn't know or care.

Educational:

Video games can be educational. Some games require reading, which motivated my six-year-old to read. Some, more sophisticated games use logic and deductive reasoning. Many create and explore new worlds that may spark a child's interest in aviation, space or computer programming.

The garden is an educational paradise. Children can learn about botany, agronomy, entomology, biology, chemistry and a host of other subjects. Encouraging your children through this process and allowing their natural curiosity to flourish will open doors to many possible career opportunities.

Summary

Young children have a natural curiosity about the world around them. With a little imagination and patience we can bring this exciting world of gardening *and fitness* to them.

Chapter Twenty-Four

A Day in the Garden

I can think of no better way to summarize *Fitness the Dynamic Gardening Way* than sharing a day in the garden with my family. Most of the concepts introduced in this book are presented in the story below. It describes a typical weekend in early summer.

I had been out of town on business, and I didn't have much time for my two children, Josh, age six, and Kristen, age three. I looked forward to spending time with them on the weekends.

It was a bright, sunny, Saturday morning. My wife, Mabel, needed to pick up some groceries at the store and went out shopping. The children and I walked into the back yard and entered the garden. It's my private oasis, teeming with life—ladybugs chomping on aphids, swallowtail butterflies darting through the air, and barn swallows eating mosquitoes by the hundreds. Red and orange zinnias, sky-blue stokesia and white aquilegia brightened up the flower garden. Crisp snow peas, deep-green broccoli and garden-fresh spinach filled the raised vegetable beds.

The children and I filled a bucket with juicy red strawberries. We picked early, vine-ripened tomatoes, radishes, and spinach.

We found some "good bugs," ladybugs, and a "bad bug," a cabbage loper caterpillar. We fed the caterpillar to a wolf spider, his web conveniently nestled in a corner of the garden.

I explained "the balance of nature" and how our garden was a microcosm of life and death. The vegetables grew from the soil.

The bad bugs ate our vegetables. The good bugs ate the bad bugs. We ate the vegetables. Whatever was left went into the compost pile, where it would transform into a brown, sweet smelling humus that would again feed the plants. We cooperated *with* nature to grow fresh fruits, vegetables, herbs and flowers.

For lunch, we ate chicken salad on a bed of spinach with fresh tomatoes, snow peas, and herbs. Dessert was juicy, flavorful, garden-fresh strawberries. My wife, Mabel, returned from shopping. In the afternoon, the family gardened together. Mabel planted flowers. Kristen and I dug up some weeds (OK, Kristen pulled up *anything* that was green but she was *so* cute doing it.) I showed Josh how to hold a hoe and cultivate the soil around the snow peas he had planted. He was so proud as they grew strong and climbed up the trellis. He called them "Jack in the Beanstalks." Josh soon tired of the garden and played with his toys.

Kristen followed me around with wide-eyed wonder. As I walked I stretched, lunged and weeded every few steps. We watched a swallowtail butterfly caterpillar eat the leaves of a parsley plant that had bolted to seed. Later, we found a chrysalis, the pupa form of a butterfly. I explained to Kristen how the odd, green shape would someday become a beautiful swallowtail butterfly. No amount of textbook reading could compare with the lesson my children learned firsthand in the garden that day. They saw, heard, smelled, touched and tasted the delights and wonders of nature.

It was time for my "workout." I grabbed a pitchfork and spent an invigorating thirty minutes moving the pile of grass clippings, leaves, dirt and table scraps from one bin to another. This mixture of materials would soon transform into compost, "black gold," the foundation of the sustainable garden. The compost had a sweet, earthy smell, like the soil found under the trees in a forest on a wet, spring day.

I purposely alternated my grip, from left-handed to right-handed, every fifteen shovelfuls. I used my legs and arms to lift the shovel loads of dirt. My neighbor watched me exercise and motioned toward his back. I smiled and thought about the millions of people who immediately think of a sore back when they think of gardening. My back didn't hurt. My leg muscles burned as I used them repeatedly to lift the dirt, but it felt good. I rested between each set of fifteen repetitions. I finished five sets of fifteen repetitions and rested. I didn't want to turn the entire pile in one day. I always saved some for later.

Kristen watched me and laughed. "Daddy dig in the dirt," she said over and over. Her blond hair glistened in the afternoon sun. As my muscles strained and the sweat poured off my brow, I remembered Kristen eating the super-sweet "Chelsea" cherry tomatoes I grew last season. Each time she bit into a tomato, the seeds and juice squirted out and ran down her cheeks. She'd laugh and ask for another one. The compost I created today would nurture the seven-foot tomato plants that provided our family with hundreds of delicious cherry tomatoes, so sweet, Kristen would prefer them to candy.

I heard the honk of a horn and turned to see my parents' car. Josh and Kristen both jumped up and ran to see grandpa and grandma. My mom looked at the flowers and smiled. My dad made a beeline for the garden. He would pick lettuce, beans, kale and whatever else he could find and eat it, raw, straight from the garden. He'd look at me and smile.

"Organic, right?" He'd rub a cherry tomato against his shirt and stuff it into his mouth.

I wasn't born on a farm—just the opposite. I was born in Brooklyn. Some of my earliest memories are of the tomato plants we grew in our small back yard. Each day, I'd search the tomato plants for the big, green caterpillars with the red tail—tomato hornworms. I would pull off some stalks and leaves, set the caterpillars on them, and watch them eat for hours. Insects always fascinated me. I always preferred watching them in their natural habitat than killing and collecting them.

Since I had company, I decided to shorten my workout. Instead of manually cultivating the garden, I used a mini-tiller. In about fifteen minutes, I cleared the paths and prepared a bed for a second planting. At the end of my workout I always did a few sets of pullups on the chinup bar over the grape arbor.

"Daddy strong" Josh said, as he watched me do three sets of eight. He flexed his little muscles. I helped Josh do five pullups.

Before dinner we went swimming for an hour at the community pool. Swimming was my cross-training complement to gardening. The cool water felt good as I exercised my muscles and worked up an appetite. Josh and Kristen enjoyed splashing and playing in the water. Grandma took pictures. Grandpa swam laps.

We returned home and prepared dinner—cabbage, tomatoes, zucchini, onions, garlic and fresh herbs, wrapped in tin foil and baked over hot coals. We had plenty of salad, a feast of greens of different colors, textures and flavors.

After dinner, Josh showed grandma and grandpa his Gi; the starched, white outfit dwarfed his slender, forty pound frame. He had just started Taekwondo a week before and was a white belt. He was so proud. He jumped and kicked in the air. My dad asked me when I'd start. I wasn't so sure, I told him. Maybe I'd try it later. (I started a month later. Within a year I was a blue belt.)

Later that night, after the children were asleep, I spent a few moments reading about perennial plants I had never grown. My eyes slowly grew tired. I felt good, alive. This warm, pleasant feeling is one that millions of gardeners and farmers experience but few can describe. My day was full, active. I had a good workout. I spent quality time with my children teaching them about the wonders and beauty of nature. We swam at the pool. The entire family enjoyed a delicious, nutritious meal we'd grown ourselves.

My body and mind were equally tired, I was at peace with myself—and soon asleep. I dreamed of the garden, how I wanted it to be and the magic moments I would enjoy with my family.

Morning came quickly, and I awoke from a deep sleep. Still groggy, I walked to the window and looked at the garden. It was still there, today, as it would be tomorrow and many years from now. I opened the front door and picked up the newspaper from the sidewalk. A jogger sprinted past, glancing at my display of flowering plants and nodded his approval. I returned to the house and sat down with my newspaper. I looked out my back window at the garden and smiled.

Chapter Twenty-Five

Summary

Fitness the Dynamic Gardening Way is a health and wellness lifestyle that engages your body, mind and spirit. The dozens of medical doctors, nutritionists and psychologists interviewed all agree—gardening is good for you.

I've dieted. I've worked out at the local health spa, I've jogged, cycled and walked. While it always felt great afterwards, mustering up the motivation to go was always a chore.

Contrasted with other health and fitness programs that *recommend* changing your lifestyle, the Dynamic Gardening Way *is a lifestyle*. Whereas previously the primary goal of gardening was to grow fresh fruits, vegetables, flowers and herbs—under the umbrella of Dynamic Gardening *what you grow* shares *equal importance* with the exercise and psychological benefits.

Dynamic Gardening also redefines fitness to include all people, regardless of their size, shape or athletic ability. It now includes children who can't make the basketball team but can be physically fit exercising in the garden and eating nutritious food; retired people sharing their wisdom and love of gardening with others; physically or mentally disabled individuals exercising, being productive and feeling good about themselves as they nurture plants; grandparents, parents, children and neighbors exercising together to create beautiful floral displays.

Gardening is fun, physical and beautiful. The secret is that everything is interconnected. One activity leads to another. Each activity yields multiple benefits. You can increase self-esteem and environmental awareness—as you learn about the wonders and mysteries of nature. If any particular activity is not for you then try another. Invent your own. Experiment. Play. Have fun. Grow something. *Anything.* Just start.

I can't guarantee you'll lose five pounds a week exercising in your garden and eating fresh fruits and vegetables. That's never been my intent. If you follow even a small portion of the ideas presented in this book, you will tone your body, eat fresh, great-tasting fruits and vegetables and feel better. More importantly, you'll discover a lifestyle that promotes health and wellness, not for a few weeks or months, but a lifetime.

I would love to hear your thoughts on *Fitness the Dynamic Gardening Way.* Let me know if you are aware of any new research or would be interested in contributing to a future edition. I would also be interested how *Fitness the Dynamic Gardening Way* has helped you achieve fitness. You may reach me through the publisher.

C/O Jeff Restuccio
Balance of Nature Publishing
P.O. Box 637
Cordova TN 38018-0637

The Dynamic Gardening Way
Summary

Healthy Lifestyle

Fun, Rewarding, Creative, Aesthetic

Psychological Well-Being

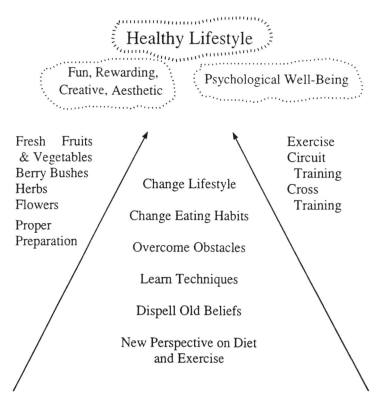

Fresh   Fruits
 & Vegetables
Berry Bushes
Herbs
Flowers

Proper
Preparation

Change Lifestyle

Change Eating Habits

Overcome Obstacles

Learn Techniques

Dispell Old Beliefs

New Perspective on Diet
and Exercise

Exercise
Circuit
 Training
Cross
 Training

A Health and Wellness Program for a Lifetime

Appendix

Sources for More Information and Supplies

Gardening Magazines:

National Gardening
National Gardening Association
180 Flynn Avenue
Burlington VT 05401

Organic Gardening
33 East Minor Street
Emmaus PA 18098

Flower & Garden
P. O. Box 7507
Read Oak IA 51591-0507

Fine Gardening
The Taunton Press
63 South Main Street
Box 9955
Newtown CT 06470-9955

HortIdeas
Route 1
P.O. Box 302
Black Lick Road
Gravel Switch KY 40328

Books:

Ball, Jeff. *Rodale's Garden Problem Solver: Vegetables, Fruits & Herbs*. Emmaus PA: Rodale Press, 1988.

Bartholomew, Mel. *Square Foot Gardening*. Emmaus PA: Rodale Press, 1981.

Encyclopedia of Organic Gardening, New Revised Edition. Emmaus PA: Rodale Press, 1978.

Creasy, Rosalind. *The Complete book of Edible Landscaping: home landscaping with food-bearing plant and resource-saving techniques*. San Francisco CA: Sierrra Club, 1982.

Denckla, Tanya. *Gardening at a Glance: The Organic Gardener's Handbook on Vegetables, Fruits, Nuts and Herbs*, Franklin WV: Wooden Angel Publishing, 1991.

Hunt, Marjorie B. and Brenda Bortz. *High-Yield Gardening*, Emmaus PA: Rodale Press, 1986.

Organic Fertilizers and Pesticides:

Nitron Industries
P.O. Box 400
Fayetteville, AR 72702
800-835-0123

Ringer Corporation
9959 Valley View Road
Minneapolis MN 55344-3585
612-941-4180

Gardens Alive
1030 Hwy 48
P.O. Box 149
Sunman IN 47041

Natural Gardening
Research Center
Hwy 48—P.O. Box 149
Sunman, IN 4701
812-623-3800

Safer, Inc.
189 Wells Ave.
Newton MA 02159
800-423-7544

Gardener's Supply Company
128 Intervale Road
Burlington, VT 05401
802-863-1700

BIO-Control
P.O. Box 337
Berry Creek CA 95916
916-589-5227

Maxicrop USA, Inc.
P.O. Box 964
Arlington Heights IL 60006

Mellinger's
2350GC Range Rd
North Lima, OH 44452

Beneficial Insectary
14751 Oak Run Rd
Oak Run CA 96069
916-472-3715

Tools, Organic Supplies and Garden Furniture:

Gardener's Supply Company
128 Intervale Road
Burlington, VT 05401
802-863-1700

Smith & Hawken
25 Corte Mader
Mill Valley CA 94941-1829
415-383-4415

Garden Tools:

True Temper
465 Railroad Ave.
Camp Hill PA 17001
717-737-1500

Ames Lawn & Garden Tools
P.O. Box 1774
Parkersburg WV 26101
800-624-2654

Langenbach Fine Tool Co.
P.O. Box 453
Blairstown NJ 07825
201-362-5886

Tillers and Chipper/-Shredders:

Mantis Manufacturing Co.
1458 County Line Rd., Dept 8106
Huntingdon Valley, PA 19006

Garden Way Inc.
102nd St. & 9th Ave.
Troy, NY 12180
518-235-6302

Amerind MacKissic
Dept. OGO28 P.O. Box 111
Parker Ford PA 19457

American Honda Motor Co. Inc.
P.O. Box 50
Gardena, CA 90247

Kemp Shredder/Chippers
Kemp Company
160 Koser Rd. Dept 11038
Lititz PA 17543
717-627-7979

Ariens Co.
655 W. Ryan St.
Brillion, WI 54110

Snapper Power Equipment
P.O. Box 777
McDonough, GA 30253

Vornado Power Products
2 Main St.
Melrose, MA 02176

Kinsman Company
Dept. 775 River Road
Point Pleasant, PA 18950
800-733-5613
215-297-5613

John Deere
1400 Third Ave.
Molina IL 61265
800-544-2122

HMC
The Green Machine
P.O. Box 560
20710 S. Alameda St
Long Beach CA 90810

BCS Mosa Inc.
P.O. Box 1739
Mathew, NC 28106

Scotchmen
RD #1
Potstown, PA 19464

Seeds and Supplies:
Park Seed
Cokesbury Rd
P.O. Box 46
Greenwood, S.C 29648-0046

Thompsen & Morgan
P.O. Box 1308A
Jackson NJ 08527-0308

Northrup King Cons. Products
P.O. Box 959
Minneapolis MN 55440

Henry Field's
Seed & Nursery Co.
Shenandoah Iowa 51602

Gurney's Seed & Nursery Co.
110 Capital
Yankton SD 57079

Harris Seeds
60 Saginaw Drive
P.O. Box 22960
Rochester NY 14622-2960

Hastings
1036 White St. S.W.
P.O. Box 115535
Atlanta GA 30310-8535
800-334-1771

Abundant Life Seed Foundation
P.O. box 772
Port Townsend WA 98368
(Heirloom varieties, $1)

Pinetree Garden Seeds
New Gloucster, ME 04260
207-926-3400
(inexpensive packets)

Johnny's Selected Seeds
Foss Hill Rd.
Albion ME 04910

W. Atlee Burpee & Co.
Warminster, PA 18974
215-674-4900

Shepherd's Garden Seeds
30 Irene St.
Torrington CT 06790
(European varieties)

Butterbrooke Farm
78 Barry Rd
Oxford CT 06483

John Curran
14 Cedar Ave
Manahawkin NJ 08050

Le Jardin Du Gourmet
P.O. Box 75
St. Johnsbury Center VT 05863
(Inexpensive seed packets)

Roses, Bulbs, Flowers & Perennials:

Jackson & Perkins
1 Rose Lane
Medford Oregon 97501
800-292-4769

Van Bourgondien Bros.
245 Farmingdale Rd.
P.O. Box A
Babylon NY 11702

Spring Hill
6523 N. Galeria Rd.
Peoria IL 61632

Fruits and Berries:

Stark Bros.
Nurseries & Orchards Co.
P.O. Box 10
Louisiana MO 63353-9985

J.E. Miller Nurseries
1605 West Lake Rd.
Canandaigua NY 14424

Outdoor Gym Equipment:

Woodplay, Inc.
P.O. Box 27904
Raleigh, NC 27611
919-231-6080

Timberworks
18036 U.S. 41
Brooksville, FL 34610
800-677-7777

Greenhouses:

Hobby Greenhouse Association
8 Glen Terrace
Bedford MA 01730-2048
Membership is $10.

The following greenhouse kits are free-standing, set apart from the house. No foundation is required, although most use pressure-treated runners and a pea gravel floor.

Hoophouse Greenhouse Kit
Fox Hill Farm
20 Lawrence St.
Vernon, CT 06006
203-875-6676
10' x 12', constructed of 6-mil polyethylene film, galvanized-steel tubing and wood. List price: $199.

Gothic Arch Greenhouses
P.O. Box 1564
Mobile AL 36633
Corrugated fiberglass, reinforced plastic and redwood and western red cedar, 8' x 12' greenhouse. List price: $995.

The Northern Light Greenhouse,
Gardener's Supply Co.
128 Intervale Road
Burlington VT 05401
Double glazed high-strength plastic and aluminum 10' x 12' greenhouse. List price: $3,495.

Garden Way Inc.
102nd St. and 9th Ave.
Troy NY 12180
800-833-6990
Glass and aluminum 8' x 12' greenhouse. List price: $1,599.

Horticultural Therapy programs:

The American Horticultural
Therapy Association (AHTA)
362A Christopher Ave
Gaithersburg, MD 20879

The "Gardening from the Heart" for Disadvantaged Youth
Program:
Mr. Lloyd Kraft
811 West Santa Fe Trail
Kansas City, MO 64145
816-942-8272

Enid A. Haupt Glass Garden:
Howard A. Rusk Institute of Rehabilitative Medicine
Ms. Nancy Chambers, HTR, Director
400 E. 34th St.
New York, NY 10016
212-763-6058

Harold Cardwell, HTR, Director
Florida Division of Blind Services
Rehabilitation Center
1111 Willis Avenue
Daytona Beach, FL 32014

Melwood Horticultural Training Center
Earl Copus, Jr., Exec. Director
5606 Dower House Road
Upper Marlboro, MD 20870
301-599-8000

Chicago Botanic Garden
P.O. Box 400
Glencoe IL 60022
702-835-8300
ATTN: Eugene Rotlert, Jr. HTR

Friends Hospital
4641 Roosevelt Boulevard
Philadelphia PA 19124
ATTN: Martha Straus, HTM
Director Horticultural Therapy
215-831-4686

Dr. Richard Mattson
Kansas State University
Dept. of Horticulture, Walters Hall
Manhattan KS 66506-4002
913-532-5686
Horticultural Therapy BS & MS degree
program

The Garden Center of Greater Cleveland
11030 East Boulevard
Cleveland OH 44106
216-721-1600
ATTN: Nancy C. Stevenson, HTR

The booklet *Gardening for the Elderly and Physically Handicapped* (#426-020) is available free from:
Dr. Diane Relf
Dept. of Horticulture
Virginia Polytechnic Institute and State University
Blacksburg VA 24061

The Growing Connection in Therapy
Georgia Ctr. for Cont. Education
The Univ. of Georgia
Athens GA 30602
404-542-1756

Providence Center, Inc.
Horticulture Program
Providence Career Center
80 West Street
Annapolis MD 21401
301-267-0701

Special Tools for Disabled Individuals:
Brookstone Company
127 Vose Farm Road
Peterborough NH 03458

Green River Tools
5 Cotton Mill Hill
Box 1919
Brattleboro VT 05301

E.C. Geiger
Box 285
Harleysville PA 19438

A.H. Hummert Seed Co.
2476 Chouteau Ave.
St Louis MO 63103

Gardener's Eden
Box 7307
San Francisco CA 94120

Smith & Hawken
25 Corte Madera
Mill Valley CA 94941

Gardener's Supply Company
128 Intervale Road
Burlington, VT 05401
802-863-1700

Selected Bibliography

Diet, Nutrition and Weight Loss

Ames, Bruce N., Profet, Margie, Gold, Lois Swirsky, "Dietary Pesticides (99.99% all natural)" *Proc. National Academie Science* 87:7777-7781.

Ames, Bruce N., Profet, Lois Swirsky, "Chemical Carcinogenesis: Too Many Rodent Carcinogens" *Proc. National Academie Science* 87:7772-7776.

Ames, Bruce N., Profet, Margie, Gold, Lois Swirsky, "Nature's Chemicals and Synthetic Chemicals: Comparative Toxicology" *Proc. National Academie Science* 87:7782-7786.

Blackburn, George L. M.D. Ph.D. "12: The Magic Number for Dieting Down to Size." *Prevention* 42:30-.

Blumenthal, Dale, "A Simple Guide to Complex Carbohydrates" *FDA Consumer* April 1989, 23:13.

Brownell, Kelly D, Ph.D. "When and How to Diet." *Psychology Today*, June 1989, pp. 40-46.

Burtis, Grace, Ph.D., R.D., Davis, Judi, M.S. R.D., and Martin, Sandra, R.N., *Applied Nutrition and Diet Therapy*. Philadelphia PA, W.B. Saunders Company 1988.

Callaway, C. Wayne, M.D., "Three Fatness Traps." *U.S. News & World Report*. 14 May 1990, p. 61.

Callaway, C. Wayne, M.D., *The Callaway Diet*. New York: Bantam, 1990.

Ferguson, James M., M.D. *Habits Not Diets*. Palo Alto: Bull Publishing Co., 1988.

Fisher, Arthur, "Fat Facts" *Popular Science*, August 1990, 237:p 26.

Fletcher, Anne M. M.S., R.D., "Thin for Life" *Prevention,* October 1990, 42:58.

Fletcher, Anne M. M.S., R.D. "Diet Breakthroughs to Keep you Younger, Longer." *Prevention,* 43:34.

Fletcher, Anne M. M.S., R.D., et al. "Finally Lose Weight—the Self-Esteem Plan" *Prevention,* 43:44.

Freundlich, Naumi, Cantrell, Wanda; Jereski, Laua; Hong, Peter, "The Great American Health Pitch" *Business Week,* 9 October 89, 3127:114.

Glamour, Editors of, "Why Your Last Diet Failed." *Glamour,* June 1989, 238-47.

Hales, Dianne, *Readers Digest* (Family Circle, Sept 5, 1989), December 1989, pp. 160-162.

Johnson, Julie, "Bringing Sanity to the Diet Craze" *Time,* 21 May 1990, 135:74.

Katahn, Martin, Ph.D. *The Rotation Diet.* New York: WW Norten and Co., 1986.

Nugent, Nancy, and the Editors of Prevention Magazine, *Food and Nutrition.* Emmaus: Rodale Press, 1984.

Olson, Susan C., Ph.D., Colvin, Robert H., Ph.D., *Keeping it Off.* New York: Simon and Shuster,1985.

Pellelt, Peter L. "Protein Requirements in Humans." *American Journal of Clinical Nutrition,* 51:1100-5.

Prevention Magazine, Editors of, *Understanding Vitamins and Minerals.* Emmaus: Rodale Press, 1984.

Prevention Magazine, Editors of, *Fitness for Everyone.* Emmaus: Rodale Press, 1984.

Segal, Marian, "Modified Fast: a Sometime Solution to a Weighty Problem" *FDA Consumer* April 1990, 24:3.

Simopoulos, Artemis P. "Nutrition and Fitness." *The Journal of the American Medical Association*, 261 (1989):2862-64.

Stephen, Allison M. and Wald, Nicholas J. "Trends in Individual Consumption of Dietary Fat in the United States, 1930-1984." *American Journal of Clinical Nutrition*, 52:457-69.

Time-Life Books, Editors of, *Wholesome Diet.* Alexandria VA: Time-Life Books, 1981.

Tyler, Varro E., Ph.D., "The Top 7 Herbs for Health" *Prevention*, 42:38-43.

Wadden, T.A.; Stunkard, A.J.; Brownell K.D.; and Day, S.C. "A Comparison of Two Very-Low-Calorie Diets: Protein-Sparing Modified Fast Versus Protein-Formula Liquid Diet." *American Journal of Clinical Nutrition*, 41:533-9.

Wadden, T.A.; Stunkard, A.J.; Brownell K.D.; Day, S.C.; Gould, R.A.; and Rubin, C.R. "Less Food, Less Hunger: Reports of Appetite and Symptoms in a Controlled Study of Protein-Sparing Modified Fast." *International Journal of Obesity*, 11:239-49.

Whelan, Elizabeth M., Dr., and Stare, Fredrick J., Dr., *The One-Hundred-Percent Natural, Purley Organic, Cholesterol-Free, Megavitamin Low-Carbohydrate Nutrition Hoax.* New York: Atheneum, 1983.

Young, Frank E. , M.D., Ph.D. "Weight Food Safety Risks." *FDA Consumer*, September 1989, 23:8-13.

Zifferblatt, Steven, M., Ph.D. "America the Fat." *Saturday Evening Post*, September 1990, 262:26.

—,"The Bulge Stops Here." *American Health*, May 1990,:54-7.

Exercise

Columbo, Franco, and Tyler, Dick, Dr., *Weight Training and Body-building*. New York: Wanderer Books, 1979.

Pearl, Bill, and Moran, Gary T., Ph.D., *Getting Stronger*. Bolinas CA: Shelter Publications, 1986.

Schwarzenegger, Arnold, and Dobbins, Bill, *Arnold's Bodybuilding for Men*. New York: Simon & Schuster, 1981.

Vedral, Joyce, L., Ph.D., *The 12-Minute Total-Body Workout*. New York: Warner Books, 1989.

Georgakas, Dan, Dr. *The Methuselah Factors*. New York: Simon and Shuster, 1980.

Gardening

Bartholomew, Mel. *Square Foot Gardening*. Emmaus PA: Rodale Press, 1981.

Daniels, Stevie. "Uninvited Guests" *Organic Gardening*, April 1989, pp. 39-42.

Denckla, Tanya. *Gardening at a Glance: The Organic Gardener's Handbook on Vegetables, Fruits, Nuts and Herbs*. Franklin WV: Wooden Angel Publishing, 1991.

Editors, of, *Encyclopedia of Organic Gardening, New Revised Edition*. Emmaus PA: Rodale Press, 1978.

Hunt, Marjorie B. and Bortz, Brenda. *High-Yield Gardening*. Emmaus PA: Rodale Press, 1986.

McGrath, Michael. "Diet Fantasy." *Organic Gardening*, June 1988, pp. 52-58.

Mott, Lawrie, and Snyder, Karen. *Pesticide Alert*. Sierra Club Books, San Fransisco CA, 1986.

Organic Gardening Magazine, Editors of, *Q & A, Hundreds of Can-Do Answers to a Gardener's Toughest Questions*. Emmaus: Rodale Press, 1989.

Pleasant, Barbara."Garden Grown Immunity: Cultivate the Foods Your Body Needs to Maintain Optimal Health." *Organic Gardening*, Sept-Oct 1990, pp. 42(5).

Stout, Ruth, *How to have a Green Thumb Without an Aching Back*. Simon & Shuster: New York, 1973.

Winter, Ruth, M.S., *Poisons in Your Food*. New York: Crown, 1991.

278 Part Nine: Appendix

Psychology

Dyer, Wayne W., Dr., *You'll See It When You Believe It.* New York: William Morrow and Company, 1989.

Landau, Elaine *Why are They Starving Themselves?* New York: Julian Messner, 1983.

LeBoeuf, Michael, Ph.D. *Imagineering.* New York: Berkeley Books, 1980.

Maltz, Maxwell, M.D., *Live and Be Free Thru Psychocybernetics.* New York: Warner Books, 1975.

Mason, L. John., Ph.D. *Guide to Stress Reduction.* Culver City CA: Peace Press, 1980.

McKay, Matthew, Ph.D., and Fanning, Patrick, *Self-Esteem* Oakland CA: New Harbinger Publications, 1987.

Moore, Bibby, *Growing with Gardening—A Twelve-Month Guide for Therapy, Recreation and Education,* Chapel Hill NC: The University of North Carolina Press, 1989.

Relf, Diane, Ph.D., "Dynamics of Horticultural Therapy", *Rehabilitation Literature,* May-June 1981, 42:5-6.

Ornstein, Robert, and Sobel, David S. Dr. "Healthy Pleasures" *Flower and Garden,* March/April 1990.

Ornstein, Robert, and Sobel, David S. Dr. *Healthy Pleasures* Reading: Addison-Wesley Publishing, 1989.

Siegel, Michele, Ph.D.; Brisman, Judith, Ph.D.; Weinshel, Margot, M.S.W. *Surviving an Eating Disorder* New York: Harper & Row, 1988.

Taylor, Mary. "The Healthy Gardener" *Flower and Garden* March/April 1990, p. 46.

Other books:

Horticultural Therapy for Nursing Homes, Senior Centers and Retirement Living, Eugene Rothert and James Daubert, 130 pp. ($10.00).

Horticultural Therapy at a Physical Rehabilitation Facility, Eugene Rothert and James Daubert, 130 pp. ($10.00)

Horticultural therapy at a Psychiatric Hospital, Eugene Rothert and James Daubert, 130 pp. ($10.00)

Horticultural Therapy for the Mentally Handicapped, Eugene Rothert and James Daubert, 130 pp. ($10.00).
- (Four books above) Available from:
  Chicago Horticultural Society
  "Books"
  Horticultural Therapy Dept.
  P.O. Box 400
  Glencoe IL 60022

Raised Bed Gardening, A Resource Manual for Patients, Families, and Professionals, Julia Beems, 1988, 52pp. ($10.00)
- Available from:
  Craig Hospital
  3425 S. Clarkson
  Englewood Co 80110
  ATTN: Materials Management

Outdoor Gardening for the Handicapped, Hort. Leaflet #51, 1981, 8pp. (No Charge)
- Available from:
  Cooperative Extension Service
  Clemson University
  Clemson SC 29631

Index

adcelerated propagation system 157, 158, 209, 248
American Horticultural Therapy Association 2, 11, 219, 221, 270
ankle weights 89
annual 114, 115, 119, 160, 162, 173, 189
antioxidants 10, 192, 193
Basal Metabolic Rate 27, 57
beneficial insects 46, 47, 145, 151, 153, 178, 236, 249, 252
green lacewing 151
ladybugs 151, 178, 253, 255
praying mantis 151, 152, 178, 252
trichogramma wasps 151
biennial 115, 160
black plastic 212
bolting 186
Callaway Diet 1, 10, 30, 31
carcinogens 191
chipper/shredder 118, 125, 138, 174, 175, 243
Circuit Training 7, 55, 61, 75, 81, 89, 90, 92, 94-96, 105, 113, 119, 243, 250
chinups 106, 110, 111, 115-117, 241
dip bar 84, 102, 103, 112, 116, 117, 243
pullups 16, 55, 61, 82, 83, 90, 91, 93, 110, 111, 115-117, 119, 257, 258
pushups 36, 40, 87, 109, 115, 116, 117, 237
roman chair 88
sit-ups 55, 61, 83, 91, 93, 115, 116, 117
cloche 165
cold frame 115, 164, 165, 169, 173

companion planting 47, 138, 145, 178
competitive sports 57, 78
complex carbohydrates 179, 180, 273
compost 1, 15, 18, 47-49, 51, 60, 61, 62, 68, 75, 90, 91, 92, 93, 106, 109, 111, 112, 113, 115, 116, 117-119, 123, 125, 126-129, 131, 132, 134, 138, 143, 165, 171, 174, 178, 181, 189, 201, 207, 211, 217, 226, 232, 235, 236, 243, 248, 249, 256, 257
air 40, 45, 50, 125-127, 134, 145, 150, 154, 173, 174, 183, 185, 186, 255, 258
ingredients 125
mass 15, 17, 27, 61, 78, 81, 126, 128, 201, 203, 238
size 125
turning 60, 61, 75, 90, 92, 109, 111-113, 125, 127, 128, 137, 138, 171, 217, 236
water 15, 25, 28, 30, 36, 63, 86, 104, 122, 125, 126, 134, 149, 150, 153, 158, 161, 165, 168, 170, 171, 173, 174, 180-185, 196, 209, 212, 240, 258
cover crops 137, 174
crop rotation 173

cultivating 51, 55, 57, 60, 68, 73, 81,
    90, 91-93, 113, 144, 210, 217,
    243, 257
cutting wood 14, 76
damping off 160
deep-dug garden beds 134, 144
definition 60, 61, 121
diet pills 28, 243
dormant oil spray 151
double digging 14, 55, 61, 75, 90, 91,
    93, 113, 129, 132, 134, 142,
    150, 156
drip irrigation 173, 212
earthworms 141, 143, 249
eating disorders 19, 200, 203
eating habits 23, 24, 27, 31, 39, 41,
    43, 46, 49, 179
edible flowers 188
exercise 1-3, 6-9, 11, 13, 14, 16, 17,
    cool down 61, 75, 79, 90, 217
    duration 61, 62, 91-93, 113, 223
        repetitions 16, 60-62, 73,
            83, 86, 250, 257
    stance 17, 55, 58, 59, 68, 69, 72,
        73, 109, 111, 112, 132, 206
    stretching 3, 47, 55, 60, 63, 64,
        67, 68, 90, 91, 93, 217, 243
    warm-up 61, 63, 79
fad diets 24, 32, 35
fertilizers 15, 18, 47, 121, 131, 141,
    142, 143, 146, 156, 178, 213,
    242, 266
fertilizers-chemical
    10-10-10 15
fertilizers-natural 13, 15, 18, 28, 30, 39,
    51, 75, 89, 121, 122, 142, 145, 150,
    153, 154, 168, 182, 191, 197, 217,
    232, 254, 257, 267, 275
    bat 142, 143, 178
    earthworm 142
    greensand 143

shredded newspaper 143,
    212
fiber 27, 28, 179, 180
four basic food groups 179
free radicals 192
frequent traveling 211
Gardening from the Heart
    Program 222
gardening problems
    clay 138, 212, 213
    geography 43, 212
    not enough daylight 210,
        213
    too much shade 210
    vacations 43, 212
gardening tools 48, 53, 241
GOSPA 237, 239
    activities 14, 18, 19, 37,
        40, 49, 50, 57, 62, 75,
        76, 79, 81, 90, 92, 94,
        113, 127, 167, 174,
        176, 210, 212, 216,
        217, 219, 220, 222,
        224, 225, 227, 228,
        230, 237-239, 243,
        246, 248, 251
    feedback 230, 237, 238
    goals 15, 19, 30, 43, 47,
        52, 62, 89, 132, 209,
        217, 221, 222, 225,
        234, 235, 237-240, 246
    objectives 19, 52, 62,
        181, 206, 217, 237-
        -239, 241, 244-246
    plans 19, 100, 237-239
    strategies 19, 47, 52, 146,
        156, 237, 238, 239,
        242, 245
    effective 73, 144-146,
        149-151, 153,

154, 155, 181, 188, 237-239
efficient 137, 238, 239
green manures 137, 173, 174
green thumb 208-210, 232, 234, 248, 277
greenhouse 96, 158, 159, 167, 213, 219, 221, 223-226, 270
hand grip 61
hardening plants off 164
herbs 49-51, 94, 114-116, 119, 138, 159, 160, 163, 164, 177, 181, 188, 189, 195, 196, 210, 213, 214, 221, 222, 240, 241, 244, 245, 246, 252, 256, 258, 261, 266, 274, 276
horticultural therapy 2, 8, 11, 19, 217, 219, 220, 221, 223, 224, 226, 227, 228-230, 240, 241, 270, 271, 278, 279
hot bed 165
hydroponics 168
insect pests 47, 68, 145, 146, 150, 151, 153, 164, 169, 209, 212, 242, 24779
interplanting 47, 138, 144, 145, 178
IPM 18, 121, 145, 150, 156, 242
landfills 15, 126, 128
LD_{50} 146-149, 154, 155
lifestyle 1-3, 5-7, 9, 13, 15, 17, 19, 20, 23, 27, 31, 37, 39, 41, 43, 49, 50, 52, 53, 55, 57, 63, 78, 89, 94, 113, 122, 123, 142, 156, 165, 167, 176, 177, 182, 192, 201, 205, 209, 217, 222, 230, 240, 250, 261-263
liquid protein 29
lunge and weed 67, 72, 136
manure 14, 48, 127, 142, 235
mechanical deterrents 150

Melwood Horticultural Training Center 10, 225, 271
minerals 31, 179, 185, 192, 274
mulch 72, 73, 115, 174, 178, 187, 211, 212, 242
muscles of the body 107, 108
abdomen 36, 112, 233
ankle 89, 112
biceps 81, 83, 106, 109, 110
deltoids 83, 86, 106, 109, 110
external oblique 106, 112
forearms 83, 109, 110
gluteus maximus 111
latissimus dorsi 76, 81, 83, 106, 111
quadriceps 106, 112
trapezius 73, 106, 111
triceps 81, 83, 87, 89, 109, 110
wrist 60, 89, 109, 110
muscles of the body—illustration
back 108
front 107
nitrogen 125, 127, 141-143, 173, 186, 189
NPK 141
organic fertilizer 16, 76
organic gardening 2, 6, 14, 15, 122, 123, 143, 150, 159, 168, 191, 205, 242, 266, 276, 277, 281
Oriental squat 71
overweight condition
psychological 200
physiological 200

perennial 47, 62, 114-117, 119, 160,
161, 163, 171, 177, 188, 210,
241, 258
perlite 161, 162
pesticides 15, 18, 47, 68, 121, 143,
144, 145, 146, 148, 150, 154,
156, 178, 190, 191, 242, 243,
266
residues 145, 146, 149, 153, 154,
184, 190, 191
toxicity 145-149, 154, 155
pesticides—natural
milky spore 153
pyrethrum 139, 155, 178
rotenone 150, 154, 155, 178
sabadilla 155
phosphorus 141, 142
physically disabled 219, 220
positive reinforcement 32, 46, 57, 248,
251
posthole digger 73, 74, 110
potassium 63, 76, 141, 187, 188
prepackaged foods 29
propagation 7, 157, 158, 163, 209,
226, 248
recycling 15, 176, 240
row cover 150, 169, 174
saturated fat 31, 197
seasons 3, 7, 13, 114, 165, 167, 172,
177, 212, 213, 242, 252
early spring 50, 90, 92, 94, 150,
151, 157, 159, 164, 168, 169,
171, 174, 176, 181, 236, 242
fall 14, 24, 50, 75, 96, 116, 127,
132, 151, 157, 159-161, 167,
168, 173, 174, 176, 178, 187,
195, 201, 241, 242
spring 50, 51, 76, 90, 92, 94, 116,
127, 132, 150, 151, 157, 159,
162, 164, 167-171, 173, 174,
176, 178, 181, 187, 195, 212,

229, 236, 241, 242,
256, 269
summer 15, 46, 50, 51,
116, 127, 134, 139,
151, 159, 167, 169,
171, 173, 174, 178,
186, 195, 196, 210,
212, 221, 241, 255
winter 14, 37, 50, 63, 75,
76, 96, 151, 157, 160,
163, 165, 167-169,
174, 176, 182, 188,
221, 240, 277
seed germination 162
self-sow 157, 163, 186
soil 14, 15, 18, 45, 47, 48, 50,
51, 75, 76, 113, 121,
122, 123, 125, 126,
128-132, 134-138,
141-145, 148, 149,
153, 154, 156, 159162,
165, 168, 170, 171,
173, 174, 178, 182,
184, 185, 186, 189,
201, 209, 211, 212,
213, 228, 236, 243,
248, 249, 252, 255,
256
acid 24, 183, 184, 192
alkaline 213
clay 132, 138, 212, 213,
229
compaction 126, 134,
144, 174
pH 141, 161, 213
special physical requirements
37, 49, 228
spreading plants 163
starting plants 18, 157, 169,
209, 235
sticky traps 145, 150

stress 1-3, 8, 11, 13, 15, 19, 23, 39, 43, 49, 52, 57, 78, 200, 214, 215, 216, 217, 233, 234, 278
stretching
  lunge 67, 72, 136
succession planting 171
sunflowers 183, 189
sustainable gardening 7, 121, 122, 141, 156
tilling 91, 93, 137, 170
tubers 157, 164, 165, 183
vacations 43, 212
vegetables 3, 7, 13, 15, 18, 19, 24, 28, 31, 39, 40, 45-50, 52, 53, 55, 68, 75, 78, 96, 97, 106, 113, 114-119, 122, 128, 136, 137, 138, 141, 144-146, 150, 162, 163, 164, 167, 168, 170-175, 177, 179-184, 186, 189-197, 201, 207, 209, 210, 211-214, 217, 221, 224, 229, 230, 232, 234, 236-238, 240-242, 244, 245, 246, 248-252, 255, 256, 261, 262, 266, 276
  Armenian cucumbers 187
  asparagus beans 187
  cherry tomatoes 186, 257
  kale 116, 171, 173, 183, 187, 193, 257
  Jerusalem artichoke 163, 164, 174, 183
  malabar spinach 186
  peanuts 184, 189, 193
  snow peas 186, 193, 195, 232, 255, 256
  Swiss chard 150, 162, 173, 181, 183, 186, 210
vermiculite 161-163
visualization 8, 19, 231, 234, 235, 243
vitamins 31, 179, 182-185, 187, 192, 196, 274

Wall O' Water 170
weeding 51, 55, 58, 62, 67, 68, 69-72, 89, 91-93, 109, 111, 112, 134, 138, 201, 206, 210, 215, 228, 236, 248, 253
weight loss 17, 23-25, 30-32, 35, 36, 46, 50, 188, 199, 200, 244, 245, 246, 273
  set point 200, 201, 203
wrist weights 89

Jeffrey P. Restuccio tests new plant varieties in the Southeast for *Organic Gardening* magazine. He is the founder and past president of the Mid-South Organic Network (MIDSON), a volunteer association dedicated to promoting the benefits of organic gardening and sustainable agriculture. MIDSON conducts organic gardening classes, maintains an organic demonstration garden at the Memphis Botanic Gardens, and works with other gardening and agricultural associations in the Mid-South area. Jeff has appeared on numerous television and radio programs promoting the health benefits of gardening.

Jeff graduated Summa Cum Laude from West Virginia University with a B.A. in psychology and has an M.B.A. from Memphis State University.

Jeff is married and lives in Cordova, Tennessee with his wife, Mabel and two children, Josh and Kristen.